A MORE SELF-CONFIDENT MAN

STRENGTHEN YOUR SELF-CONFIDENCE BY ELIMINATING NEGATIVE BELIEFS, FEARS, AND FRUSTRATIONS.

ANDREW GLOVER

BRICKTOP PUBLISHING

CONTENTS

INTRODUCTION

Our life is what our thoughts make it.

— MARCUS AURELIUS

You probably think that some people have it easy in life. Some men, in particular, appear to carry with them an air of natural self-confidence that seems to get them anything they want: partners, money, jobs, titles, and so on. What if I told you that you can build confidence and attain your goals to be like these men? Confident men are not born; they are made. I was painfully shy as an adolescent, so was Theodore Roosevelt. I reinvented myself in college to be a more confident man. Roosevelt took up boxing and became the 26th President of the United States. You are probably not running for president (neither am I), rather you are trying to attract a partner, get a better job, and build a legacy. Perhaps your lack of confidence is getting in the way of your success. If so, this book is for you.

If you suffer from low self-confidence, you are not alone. Jennifer Guttman (2019) reports that 85% of people worldwide have low self-esteem (the difference between confidence and esteem will be elucidated later). Low self-esteem is linked to violent behavior, suicide, low academic achievement, and other negative outcomes. The World Health Organization estimates that there are more deaths worldwide caused by suicide than homicide and war combined (Guttman, 2019). There is an epidemic of people with insufficient positive feelings about themselves, and this contributes to a dysfunctional society and a stunted economy. Women experience low self-confidence at fairly high rates. For instance, Guttman (2019) observes that 78% of 17-year-old girls report being unhappy with their bodies. In some ways, men fare better in this metric, but men's self-confidence is related to other facets of life that are relatively difficult to measure: responsibility, reputation, and honor. There is less explicit support for men's mental health issues in practice and in the literature. The plight of men goes relatively unnoticed. Men routinely die in wars, and we build the buildings that we bomb (and also defend); as such we are relatively replaceable. If you are reading this, then you are a man (most likely) trying to find self-confidence in a rapidly changing world, where the markers of confidence are increasingly removed from traditional gender roles.

Guttman contends that low self-confidence among men and women is related to what psychologists call *self-concept*. Self-concept is basically how you see yourself. If you ask yourself the question, "Who am I?," you may respond, "I am a man," "I am a father," "I am a good friend," "I am a construction worker," "I am a church pastor," and so forth. Maybe your responses are not so positive, but in any case, they are linguistic interpretations of our realities. We need a stable sense of identity in order to have self-esteem, and this leads to self-confidence (and self-actualization). Self-esteem is present-focused, which means it relates to how you see yourself now, while self-confidence relates to how you see yourself in the future. Regarding the word esteem, self-concept can be divided into three categories:

- Ideal self: The ideal self is the person you want to be. This person has the attributes or qualities you are either working toward or want to possess. It's who you envision yourself to be if you were exactly as you wanted.

- Self-image: Self-image refers to how you see yourself at this moment in time. Attributes like physical characteristics, personality traits, and social roles all contribute to your self-image.
- Self-esteem: How much you like, accept, and value yourself all contribute to your self-concept. Self-esteem can be affected by a number of factors—including how others see you, how you think you compare to others, and your role in society.

Abraham Maslow attests that self-actualization, wherein you (in Friedrich's Nietzsche's [1974] terms) "become who you are," is the pinnacle of human achievement, and this state of being is only possible when the other needs of the individual are met, such as hunger, thirst, love, and safety (Guttman, 2019). Esteem, according to Guttman (2019) is the means by which self-confidence "continues on the path to self-actualization." If you have esteem for yourself, it will build confidence. You cannot build self-confidence and self-esteem without knowing who you are. As such, self-confidence cannot be driven by external sources, or it will be fragile. Self-confidence comes from inside of you. This book will teach you how to look inside yourself for your self-confidence.

There are a number of symptoms that may present themselves if you have low self-esteem or low self-confidence. See below if any of these experiences are familiar to you:

- Are you sensitive to criticism?
- Are you socially avoidant or isolating yourself from others?
- Do you have negative thoughts about yourself or your abilities?
- Do you find difficulty in challenging and asserting yourself?
- Do you have trouble making eye contact or using confident posture?

In the coming chapters, I will provide detailed strategies that you can employ to increase your confidence, but, for now, you can consider the following actions as a start to building confidence internally:

- Verbally assert yourself to family members, friends, and others for practice.
- Take an inventory of your strengths.
- Do something new or challenging daily or weekly.
- Actively practice self-praise.

- Be honest about realistic goals to avoid disappointment.
- Improve your posture; practice good eye contact and standing straight.
- Think of what you're proud of each day.
- Stop comparing or contrasting yourself to others; focus on self-improvement from within, not without.

I described the epidemic of low self-confidence as vast. A report by The Body Shop reveals that about half (54%) of the people surveyed felt more self-doubt than self-love ("Self-love index," 2022). Those with greater self-love were able to bounce back from trauma more quickly and were less impacted by the COVID-19 pandemic. Likewise, one in three people using social media for two or more hours reported having the lowest self-love ("Self-love index," 2022). Social media's effect on self-confidence is tricky to quantify; among women, social media has been consistently, though weakly, demonstrated to be negative (Kelly et al., 2019). Among men, the results are less conclusive. Clearly, there are a lot of factors competing for our interest and time, and developing a stable self-concept (which involves building on our identity with esteem to achieve self-confidence) looks increasingly remote in the modern age. This is not so, however. As Seneca states, "Lack of confidence is not the result of difficulty. Difficulty comes from a lack of confidence" ("Seneca the Younger...," 2022). We simply don't know until we try. You are ready to try, which is why you're reading this book.

I understand what you're going through; you are looking for practical advice that will help you succeed as a man in a society increasingly less disposed to traditional male gender roles. It is valuable to retain what makes men men, and nowhere in this book do I put men down for the incredible achievements that we have been responsible for (though also horrors). At the same time, one sign of masculinity is a quiet confidence in the face of adversity; we can keep being men in a new society where an increasing diversity of gender presentations is permitted.

I described that I was somewhat of a wimpy kid. Studies reveal that childhood experiences are formative to your personality as an adult (Guttman, 2019). However, there are notable exceptions to this rule that are worth mentioning. Thomas Edison attended school for only three months and had fragile health before he became a world-famous inventor. Thomas Sowell was a slow learner in a dysfunctional home before he joined the Marines and became an economist. The aforementioned Roosevelt ignored his doctor's advice to avoid physical activity and thrived physically and politically. Mahatma Gandhi was timid, shy, and afraid of the dark but still led his country to independence.

Ralph Waldo Emerson, a prolific author who, nonetheless, suffered from poor health and was not a very good student, states that "to be yourself in a world that is constantly trying to make you something else is the greatest accomplishment," and "self-trust is the first secret to success" ("Ralph Waldo Emerson...," 2022). Emerson is right to have trust; you are reading this book because you trust yourself to take in this information and make the correct judgment. I believe, quite strongly, that the correct judgment for you is to transform yourself into a more confident man, and the means to do so is explained in this book. The journey will not be easy, but it is worth it. As Robert Frost (2022) writes, "I took the [road] less traveled by / And that has made all the difference."

1

UNDERSTANDING THE INS AND OUTS OF SELF-CONFIDENCE

Y ou are looking down the road less traveled; this road leads to increased self-confidence and a new you. You want to take it, but you're not sure. Many authors who write about how to improve your life do not inform you that your current habits—which can include depressive thinking, isolation, or dissociation—are "addictive" coping mechanisms and, in a way, easy. These old habits have their own endorphin responses; sometimes, sadness feels good (as anyone who has enjoyed an Elliott Smith record knows). So, the regular road looks appealing for this reason: you have taken it before. You know the exit out to the McDonalds. Suzanne Lachmann attests that self-confidence leads to increased positivity, happiness, and resilience. Most importantly, self-confidence is correlated with taking more risks. For men, this is especially important (since men are natural risk-takers). Without risks, there are no rewards. As Lachmann (2013, para. 12) puts it, "Circumstances have no chance of improving if you don't take action." Therefore, come with me down Frost's road, and I bet that a more self-confident man will emerge from the other side of this forest.

I described in the Introduction that the source of self-confidence is internal. That is, self-confidence is built from self-esteem—personal achievements and successes that line up with your values. The way self-confidence presents to the outside world is an attitude wherein you value yourself and feel worthy, even if you don't succeed. Self-confidence gives you a feeling of control over your life and a trust in your abilities to overcome challenges. Critically low or high self-confidence is rarely based on ability but on perspective. Low self-confidence is characterized by perceptions of self-doubt, passivity or submissive behavior, trouble standing up for your beliefs, perceptions of inferiority, and sensitivity to criticism. If this sounds like you, then you sound like me. At least, you sounded like me before I conquered the inner doubt that was leading to low self-esteem and low self-confidence.

In this chapter, I will describe systematically how to challenge the nagging thoughts and ruminations that make us believe we're not good enough or don't deserve what we have. Before that, though, I want to recommend a starting approach: express your feelings, beliefs, and needs directly and respectfully. Men are in a tough place with self-expression; on the one hand, we are often firm and direct in our speaking. We are no-nonsense, and if we say something, chances are that we mean it, and it's true. On the other hand, men are discouraged from expressing emotions, even if they are true and sensible. Honesty starts with being honest with yourself. It is hard to evaluate yourself objectively —if not impossible—but there is a perspective out there that is truer than others. It is best to adopt this perspective. Starting from a position of being as honest as possible—with yourself and others—generates self-confidence because hiding who you are will only breed self-doubt.

Related to the above point, learn how to say "no" to things you don't want to do or are unnecessary. Men are expected to please people (often including women); we hold open doors, reach things from top shelves, crack open pickle jars, fix sinks, and so forth. Sometimes, this is done at the expense of our own mental health (and certainly our time). Because we are discouraged from speaking about our feelings, we bottle it up.

This is a recipe for disaster in the long run, especially when these feelings reemerge in ways that are less productive and more destructive.

Previously, I stated that self-esteem, which results from measurable successes, builds self-efficacy (mastery) and, therefore, self-confidence. Moving forward, I will use the terms self-esteem and self-confidence interchangeably. Self-efficacy, on the other hand, is different from both terms in that it relates specifically to an individual's beliefs about their capacity to influence events in their own lives. Therefore, self-efficacy is a more future-focused concept than either self-esteem or self-confidence. You want high self-esteem or self-confidence in the moment because then you can react to a situation appropriately, but you want self-efficacy over the course of your life so that doubt becomes increasingly impossible because of all of your successes.

Common sources for feelings of self-efficacy include mastery experiences (the successes I mentioned), social models (seeing your peers succeed), and social persuasion (receiving verbal support for your capabilities). You want to be surrounded by people who are succeeding and also want to see you succeed. Self-confidence comes from an individual's trust in their own actions. Because to trust oneself or anyone else requires you to be honest, self-confidence is a realistic goal as well as a social one. Anthony Bandura (Harris, 2022, para. 2) attests, "I can be supremely confident I will fail an endeavor." This statement requires honesty. I can be confident that I will lose to Michael Jordan in a game of basketball, even though he is approaching 60 years of age. I am confident that *no* amount of training will allow me to win a game against Jordan, but maybe I can sneak in a two-pointer if I train hard enough. Therefore, if I score two points against Jordan's 98, that is a tremendous success and an example of mastery. It is a realistic goal, which is also challenging, and one I am happy with whether I succeed or not.

Confucius states that to know what something is, we must know it by its name, and we also must know what it is not. What does a self-confident man look like? Inversely, what does a man with low self-esteem look like? Below you will see some characteristics of a confident man and, later, a man with low self-esteem.

A confident man

- does what he thinks is right, even if it is unpopular.
- takes risks.
- admits mistakes and learns from them.
- accepts compliments.
- looks on the bright side of life.

There are several characteristics of people (men in particular) that are sometimes mistaken for confidence but are rooted in insecurity; among these are arrogance. Being overly confident in one's abilities while craving admiration is narcissism, not confidence. Relatedly, arrogance requires external validation, while self-confidence comes from within. A man who is truly self-confident is proud of his accomplishments without boasting about them. The Bible, to name one source of traditional wisdom, recognizes the difference between confidence and arrogance. In Matthew 6:1, Jesus declares, "Be careful that you don't do your charitable giving before men, to be seen by them, or else you have no reward from your Father who is in heaven" (*English Standard Version Bible*, 2001, Matt. 6:1). To exit the forest along Frost's road a more self-confident man, you have to calibrate your actions to your internal values. The opinions of others matter very little in the end. Friedrich Nietzsche titled his autobiography *Why I Am So Wise*, in part, because he was broadly dismissed and slandered by his contemporaries. Michelangelo, who painted *The Creation of Adam* and sculpted *David*, likely did not need to inform anyone he was a good painter and sculptor; he just did it.

A self-confident man is a risk-taker who is, nonetheless, sensible to the needs of others. Paradoxically, increased self-confidence will lead to decreased self-consciousness and promote a mindful outlook—but I will get to this more later. For now, here are the signs of a man with low self-esteem:

- He says negative things about himself and is overly critical of himself.
- He jokes about himself negatively.
- He focuses on negativity and ignores achievements.
- He blames himself when things go wrong.
- He thinks other people are better than him.
- He thinks he doesn't deserve to have fun.
- He does not accept compliments.
- He avoids challenges for fear of failing.
- He is overly upset by disapproval or criticism.
- He feels sad, depressed, anxious, ashamed, angry, or worthless.

I will skip the part about asking you if these signs are familiar in favor of simply stating that most, or all, of these characteristics are familiar to me. Knowing this, where does low self-esteem come from? Lachmann offers some sources of low self-esteem and self-confidence, including:

- *Disapproving authority figures*: Perhaps nothing you did was good enough for your parents or caregivers. Perhaps you were criticized no matter what you did, good or bad. Sometimes, I felt like my parents wouldn't care if I cured cancer because I didn't do it fast enough. The thing about self-confidence is that it is internal. Your upbringing is crucial to your personality, but it does not set your future in stone either. I was able to have successes that built up my self-esteem and self-confidence without having the approval of my parents. Kevin Coval recalls his father disapproving of his beat poetry; then, one day, his father simply showed up to Coval's performance and appreciated it. Recall that people tend to "chill out" as they age, including your parents or caregivers.

- *Uninvolved or preoccupied caregivers*: Perhaps you had parents or caregivers that did not pay attention to you, who acted as if your greatest accomplishments were not worth noticing. This kind of upbringing may make you feel "forgotten, unacknowledged, unimportant, and not accountable to anyone" (Lachmann, 2013, para. 3). Perhaps you apologize for your own existence; I did a little bit of that. Again, just because your parents or caregivers were disapproving or uninvolved does not mean they will dictate your life at 34, 24, or even 18. We are put in a position in life because of where we are born and who we are. We do not have to *stay* there.

- *Authority figures in conflict*: Perhaps your parents or caregivers fought. This is a common experience for many people. Children absorb behaviors from their parents or caregivers, and it may make them feel that they somehow contributed to the fight. Trauma, as I describe below as another source of low self-esteem and self-confidence, affects us in a myriad of ways that are challenging to measure because they compound in their effects. Being exposed to conflict is a mild-to-moderate version of trauma, and it can contribute to low self-esteem and low self-confidence if it is not challenged with personal successes independent of the familial relationship.

- *Bullying (with unsupportive parents or caregivers)*: Bullying is a common source of low self-esteem and self-confidence, so much so that it occupies three spots on this list. I was bullied by a guy I tried to be friends with. It's not something I think about often, but it's something that can stick with you if it happens repeatedly. Having unsupportive parents or caregivers when you are being bullied may lead to you feeling that anyone who befriends you is doing you a favor. This is a bad disposition because you have value in yourself, and no one is doing anyone a "favor" by hanging out with you.

- *Bullying (with over-supportive parents)*: Bullying affects us in a variety of ways, similar to trauma and conflict. Having over-supportive parents or caregivers when being bullied may make the perspective your parents or caregivers instill into you conflict with the world. As such, you may consider yourself a victim, even if you are not. This is a bad perspective to take as a man because the world will not give you anything—you have to take it. Playing the victim may work in certain circumstances, but it does not work in the long run, and it is not befitting of a self-confident man either.

- *Bullying (with uninvolved parents or caregivers)*: Bullying in this context may make you feel undeserving of notice and unworthy of attention. You may have felt scared to ask your parents or caregivers for help and resent their uninvolvement. Perhaps this led to isolation. Like the other sources of low self-esteem and self-confidence on this list, nothing about bullying with uninvolved parents or caregivers ensures that the isolation you experience needs to be permanent.

- *Academic challenges without parental or caregiver support*: School is a struggle for many of us; even if we do well, we may not "fit in." Maybe we fit in but don't do well. Maybe we don't do well and don't fit in. In any case, without parental or caregiver support in this circumstance, you may feel defective due to your underperformance. You excessively doubt your smartness. This habit is anathema to being a self-confident man because a significant part of convincing people you know what you are talking about is looking like you know what you are talking about. I will discuss this more later.

- *Physical, sexual, or emotional abuse*: Abuse is among the most traumatic experiences a man or woman can experience. A victim of abuse finds it very hard to "like" the world, to trust themselves, or to trust others. If you were abused, you may think you were complicit or somehow to blame. Perhaps you developed unhealthy coping strategies as a result, like drug or alcohol abuse. There is a way out of the forest (as a more self-confident man), even if you meet a few vipers along the way.

- *Belief system*: Perhaps you were raised in a fundamentalist household where you were told you were perpetually sinning. Maybe you feel shame, guilt, inner conflict, and self-loathing as a consequence. One tendency this source of low self-esteem and self-confidence brings is zero-sum thinking; either something is all good or all bad in this paradigm. In reality, we are often going to fall into a "gray area" between the two extremes. Examining your belief system may make you more sensitive to the needs of others and, therefore, make you a more self-confident man.

- *Society and the media*: Modern society and mass communication has set unrealistic expectations of beauty, particularly for women. Men are affected by this distortion insofar as we pursue relationships with women; we are often disappointed, while women are anxious. Moreover, men are expected to hold certain roles in society as well. There are high expectations for us too, even if they are unrelated to beauty. The ubiquity of the media ensures that, whatever these expectations for men are, there is no relief from the feelings of inadequacy when you turn on the TV or look at your phone.

I know what you're thinking: "Thanks for telling me where my problems come from, Andrew. How do I fix them, though?" First, you should know that high self-esteem is associated with better health, improved social life, increased protection against mental disorders, uptake of healthy coping strategies, and improved mental well-being. Children do better in school and report higher job satisfaction later in life when they are more confident (Lachmann, 2013). I will not go so far as to say that your entire self-identity is linguistic and stems from the self-concept we tell ourselves we are from the Introduction. However, I will say language is a big part of it. Training yourself to be more confident may actually lead to tangible improvements in your life, which will lead to even more self-confidence, self-esteem, and self-efficacy.

Eric Ravenscraft (2016) echoes advice I gave earlier in this chapter when he says to be "hyper-honest" with yourself and reasonably honest with other people. For instance, say your coworker asks you what you did this weekend. Perhaps you listened to Richard Wagner's operas, cleaned your apartment, read the Bible, and took buses in a loop around town to people-watch. For some reason, you think this is a weird set of activities.

Maybe you should have been watching *Game of Thrones.* A self-confident man will say, "Yeah, I took city buses for a sightseeing trip after finishing Jeremiah." If you have a hard time admitting to others what you do, either stop doing that thing or (better yet) accept that you do it. Stop hiding who you are. Nietzsche attests that you become who you are by facing your greatest spiritual battles; there is no growth without conflict. There is no resilience without first knowing failure. If you fail once, you can fail again better the next time, as Samuel Beckett quips.

Ravenscraft offers five more tips to gain self-confidence that are worth sharing in detail:

- *Start working out.* Exercise does wonders for anxiety, and the self-confidence follows not only from the chemical endorphins, but from the fact you look better too. Much is made about the expectations of beauty for women (as mentioned above). Men who maximize their physical stature (regardless of how they look starting out) will also maximize their social capital. A man who is physically fit tells the world, "I have discipline and confidence." Beyond training yourself mentally, training yourself physically is an essential step to building self-confidence.

- *Try things that make you uncomfortable.* I alluded earlier that the best goal you can set for yourself is one that is hard but not impossible. I have a friend who says, "You have to aim for the stars if you want to land on the Sears Tower." The Sears Tower, now named the Willis Tower, was among the tallest buildings in the world at the time he said that. Landing among the stars is impossible, but landing on the Sears/Willis Tower is only improbable. Aim for what is hard enough to do that it will bring you satisfaction if you complete it, but not so hard that you will pull your hair out if you fail. As Barbara Markway (2018) puts it, "Taking more shots means making more of them." Remember, a self-confident man is satisfied whether he succeeds or fails. The journey *is* the destination.

- *Try a new look.* I can't tell you how important this tip is. Women have a wide diversity of what "looks good" in various contexts. Men have only a certain set of classic styles. Any man will look better in a suit, with a fresh shave or a trimmed beard, and cologne that complements his look and demeanor. Research studies have demonstrated that people put more trust into those who are dressed in professional attire, such as a doctor's gown (Markway, 2018). I guarantee that a good look will engender confidence if you back it up with words and actions to match.

- *Defy imposter syndrome.* Imposter syndrome makes us think that we don't deserve what we have, like somehow we we are unique in our incompetence. We may think that anyone else can do this job but us (even though we get paid for it). A way to challenge this cognitive distortion is to be more mindful and, therefore, more self-confident; we are not really that unique in our individual failures and successes. Everyone has failures and successes, most of which we do not know about. Furthermore, everyone is good and bad at certain things. We are where we are because we are more good at certain things than some and less good than others. Remind yourself that everyone experiences imposter syndrome the next time you are ruminating about how no one else is ruminating about their lives.

- *Adjust your posture!* Stand straight, put your chest out, and raise your head. As Lou Reed (1970) sings, "Ever since I was a baby on my momma's knee… My mama told me hold your head up high."

I described how increased self-confidence will lead to less fear and anxiety and will make you more mindful (including of others' needs). Self-confidence will "quiet your inner critic," in the words of Markway (2018). Perhaps you think often about your failures and ignore your successes. Focus on those successes; it took a lot of perseverance to get to where you are today. It's not easy being a man. I had near-death experiences; I've lost all my money; I've made (even more) mistakes (as we all have). I wouldn't trade my experiences for a charmed life partying on yachts because then I would have no resilience to challenges and no personality to speak of. Remember, self-confidence comes from within and arrogance from without. Yes, I can have beautiful women on a yacht tell me I'm great, but what worth is it if I'm not really great? Furthermore, a self-confident man needs no one to validate him (besides himself), not even a beautiful woman.

Increased self-confidence will lead to increased resilience, or what Nassim Nicholas Taleb calls *antifragility*. Antifragility can be differentiated from resilience because, in this concept, you actually improve your capabilities with each setback (like a computer program that uses Boolean algebra). As Nietzsche (1974) puts it, "Whatever does not kill me makes me stronger." This was just as true when it was repeated by Conan the Barbarian.

Increased self-confidence will lead to healthier relationships. I already stated that a confident man is less focused on himself; in fact, he is probably trying to make himself useful to his community. A self-confident man is relaxed but also alert. This superficially relaxed state will put others at ease and give you social capital. Finally, you will develop deeper empathy with greater self-confidence. Books for men often ask you to either embrace your inner "barbarian" or get overly in touch with your feelings. This book does neither; by gaining self-confidence, you become more thoughtful but less emotional.

Now is the time to drop all pretense of an excuse and follow me to the next chapter, where I will help you become a more self-confident man by itemizing your strengths (and recognizing your weaknesses), but first, I want to recount a story.

2

IDENTIFYING AREAS OF
STRENGTH AND IMPROVEMENT

I had a friend, Alex, who was not a self-confident man. Yet, he had a lot to be self-confident about; Alex completed a Ph.D. in chemistry and worked in a lab inventing medication for Alzheimer's. Alex was also an accomplished musician; he played the violin and, at one point, tried out for the Chicago Symphony Orchestra (though he did not earn the spot). What was Alex self-conscious about? He got a tattoo of a dragon on his chest when he was 18. He thinks it looks stupid now, and for some reason, this tattoo has hampered his dating prospects, according to him. I asked Alex whether his accomplishments in science offset his choice to get a tattoo. He wasn't sure. I asked him whether he would give up his Ph.D. and his career if he could go back in time and not get the tattoo, and he wasn't sure about that either.

There is a lot to comment on regarding whether our lives are determined for us or if we choose our lives for ourselves. In Alex's high-level physics classes in college, he may have learned about the Block Universe, a current scientific hypothesis wherein the future has already taken place and we are simply "stepping" into it. In the case of this hypothesis, Alex decided to get a dragon tattooed on his chest before he was even born. You ask a guy like me—who started life as a puny kid and transformed himself into a self-confident man— and I say that our lives are clearly ours for the taking; this is what is called the Arrow of Time hypothesis. The tension between these two conceptions of life (our radical freedom and the outside forces that compel us to act a certain way) is both our prison and our salvation. In this paradox, I see a challenge of being authentic on the part of a man but also a potential to belong to a community much greater than ourselves. A fundamental part of being a man is accepting our responsibility to others, typically our partners and children, but also the community at large.

Individuals with low self-confidence downplay their accomplishments and fixate on their so-called "failures." In Alex's case, his "failure" was a decision to permanently mark a mythical creature on his chest. I don't view it as a failure because I think the tattoo's cool. From my perspective, Alex is a guy with a Ph.D. and a cool tattoo. However, the cognitive distortion of low self-confidence compels Alex to view his whole life as a failure, even though he may ultimately save someone else's life through his research. I wonder if the person for whom Alex's research benefits, such as by their life being extended or being cured of a disease, cares about Alex's tattoo, but I doubt it. Alex cannot remove his tattoo (at least not without pain), just like many of us cannot change other aspects of ourselves (such as who we are or where we were born). Alex may have made a choice to get the tattoo, but since there's nothing he can do about it now, Alex must accept the dragon tattoo like I would accept a missing limb if I had a freak work accident. Thankfully for Alex, the tattoo's cool, and it's *just* a tattoo.

If you can't tell, I'm not partial to the Block Theory hypothesis and prefer the Arrow of Time. Personally, I see the power individuals have to choose and how much these choices affect others. William James calls choices that really make a difference in people's lives (yours and others') "genuine options" (De Waal, 2005). The universe is full of genuine options and real possibilities. In the universe that I contend we live in, individuals are subject to habits, but we can change these habits. We can choose to pursue goals and have accomplishments. We celebrate these accomplishments. We motivate ourselves. We make ourselves better. We improve our families and communities.

Jodi Clarke (2021, para. 4) remarks that "celebrating success sets you up for future success." Pride—despite its potential excess as *hubris*—is one of the few emotions that can generate success as its outcome, though you must be careful to not let pride be your downfall. After all, it is legitimate to be proud of who you are, what you have done, and even what has been gifted to you.

The goals that we set in life and choose to pursue contribute to our self-confidence. For instance, a goal with a tangible outcome produces a reward. Say you study for a test and earn an A+. Your motivation to study for the exam is twofold if you are a self-confident man; a self-confident man studies to get the A+ and because there is intrinsic value in studying itself.

What is called *extrinsic motivation* is an extremely powerful tool for getting people to do the right thing. For instance, I am motivated to study partially because this activity pays off in the long run; I will potentially get a better job. I do not steal from stores because one consequence is going to jail, to say nothing of the moral dimension. However, the moral dimension (such as in the theft example) ties into the *intrinsic motivation* of human beings, or what we do for the sake of it. I do not steal, intrinsically, because I know it is wrong. I study, intrinsically, because I value learning. I will offer a relatively controversial statement here: I think a self-confident man does everything intrinsically because what is external becomes internal for him; he savors the process even if the process is not worth savoring. I will speak about this more later.

In this chapter my goal is for you to be able to appreciate your strengths and evaluate your weaknesses. Before I get to that, however, I want to make a note about celebrating your successes. I don't think we take enough time every day to acknowledge what we have done right and even make a little mental "party" out of it. As I mentioned earlier, human beings are tied up with other people, and men especially have a responsibility for the well-being of others. Our successes are only possible because of our community, which includes other men, but also women and children. Take time not only to appreciate yourself, but the people around you; don't forget the people who helped you in life and tell them you value them. People like feeling genuinely appreciated, as I'm sure you do too. Consider celebrating the following activities:

- having a dinner party with friends
- walking or jogging in the park
- watching a sunrise or sunset
- having a game night with friends
- seeking out a new adventure
- starting a hobby

Can any of these things be done more or less "well"? That is, is "success" in any of these activities worth celebrating (such as watching a sunset)? I argue that the answer is yes. There are people in this world who will look at a sunset and think about spreadsheets. A self-confident man does not do that. There are some people who spend a dinner party talking about themselves. A self-confident man does not do that either. There are some people that cheat at board games. I think you get the idea.

In the pursuits that you find yourself involved with in life, whether they are passions or obligations, you can ask yourself the following questions (in parentheses I relate the answers to watching a sunset):

- What did I enjoy most about this journey? (*the orange of the sunset in the sky*)
- What did I do well? (*I didn't think about anything besides the sunset.*)
- What strengths did I use? (*mindfulness*)

- What skills did I gain? (*peace of mind*)
- What do I feel most confident about? (*my ability to enjoy nature without mental interruption from intrusive thoughts*)
- How did I overcome obstacles along the way? (*I guided my thoughts away from anxieties and toward the present moment, and I accepted the thoughts and did not dwell on them if they did arise.*)
- What would I change for next time? (*I would get something to eat beforehand, so my hunger does not distract me.*)

This chapter involves asking yourself some pointed questions, reflecting on past events, and anticipating future ones. This type of thinking may be unbecoming for a self-confident man, only for the reason that a self-confident man practices mindfulness; he is in the present and has attachment only to which he cares about in the world (I will talk about Care, with a capital "c," a little later). This level of self-examination is meant to free you from the persistent rumination you may experience on an ongoing basis. Sometimes, repeating a thought (or "leaning in" to it) can be the trick to helping you accept it.

Now that you have thought about one of your journeys (such as my "journey" of watching a sunset), I want you to think about what you learned along the way. Ask yourself, "What am I good at?" If you are struggling to come up with a list of skills, then the best way to get these thoughts down is to write them out on paper. On a sheet of paper, state

- what empowers you
- what comes to you naturally
- what you were good at as a child
- what compliments people give you (that you tend to ignore)
- what skills you have that have helped you overcome challenges in the past

Maggie Wooll makes an important distinction between what empowers us and what we're good at. "While many people spend time doing what they're good at," she writes, "you may be good at what brings you down" (Wooll, 2022, para. 3). That is, maybe I'm good at differential calculus, but maybe I don't like to do it. Wooll offers good advice to those starting out on their journey to increased self-confidence, but it should be stressed that, for a self-confident man who has refined his sensibilities, what we're good at is what we like to do and what we like to do is what we're good at. At least, that is the general rule.

Wooll divides what we're good at into three categories:

- innate talent (e.g. painting, sports, math, and so forth)
- knowledge base
- recognition

My innate talent is writing. Maybe you disagree, but I do write books. My knowledge base is my understanding of mental health practices, motorcycles, 20th century French philosophy, and gardening. My recognition is the fact that you are reading my book and trusting my authority. If I were ever in a postapocalyptic scenario, I know I would be able to tell you that your thoughts are not your feelings (per CBT), fix your bike or motorcycle, quip that, per Jean-Paul Sartre, "hell is other people," and plant and harvest our dinner (Ambrisino, 2014). These skills are not exceptional; some people are welders and survivalists. Some people program computers. Others can build a boat or a house (I can build a hut). I also have a sense of humor. A sense of humor will carry you far, whether you are in a postapocalyptic scenario, as described above, or just experiencing your day-to-day grind of living in a city.

I mentioned skills here, but did I mention passions? Wooll differentiates skills from passions because, when one has a passion, skill level is not important; participation is interest-based, and participation is intrinsically motivated. Let us say that I'm not good at painting, but it is my passion. In a way, this is true. I find painting extremely relaxing, although I seem to lack the hand-eye-coordination to paint a convincing landscape (though I can apply the same skill when I fix motorcycles—see the distinction?). I repeat that while I appreciate Wooll's very-real differentiation between skills and passions, the advice for the self-confident man is only slightly tailored; we do not have much time to do things on a whim. We have responsibilities. When we choose to pursue a passion, it is best to make it into a skill.

There are many types of skills you can have, so if you have not been able to come up with many skills (or strengths) yet, consider how skills can be differentiated. *Hard skills* are those that can be measured or assessed; they include schooling, field training, and work experience. For instance, a handyman knows how to put up drywall, lay pipes, mortar bricks, and paint houses. To do this work, they have to do basic math, draw blueprints, and (often) take training courses to receive certifications. At the same time, handymen (like all other professionals) also have *soft skills.*

Soft skills include a person's capacity to nurture social relationships, help individuals get along, and employ creativity and adaptability. As Wooll (2022, para. 21) puts it, "You may be the best teacher at school, but if you treat people badly, it doesn't matter."

Have you come up with what you're good at yet? I hope so. Wooll offers a few strategies you can employ to help generate this list:

- Think about skills or actions that helped you succeed in the past.
- Take notes about how you spend your free time. Try journaling. (Hint: what you do in your free time is maybe what you're good at.)
- Ask others for their opinion about what you're good at.
- Look for patterns in your life where success followed certain actions.
- Keep an open mind as to what your real strengths are.
- Take a skills assessment.
- Go explore the world and see what "sticks."
- Hire a career coach.
- Try lots of things (and keep doing the things that work).
- Stop overthinking.

If you're like me, you probably have a hard time listing your strengths. I recommend that you acknowledge the positives in your life. Your achievements are not a case of "getting lucky;" we all get lucky (sometimes), but few of us put in work. The difference between a passion and a skill is the work put into it.

Thinking differently about yourself and acting differently as a consequence can retrain or "rewire" your brain through a mechanism known as *neuroplasticity*. I will talk more about that in another chapter. For now, I think it's best to focus on how, in the words of Hyma Pillay (2014), you can "leverage" your strengths no matter what your strengths are. As she puts it, "Your weakness is not your downfall...[it is] not something you lack, but something to develop and build" (Pillay, 2014, para. 4). She touches on an important point, which is whether it is best to focus on your strengths or try to develop your weaknesses (assuming one cannot do both). I side with Pillay in her contention that one should focus on their strengths. The reality is that "focusing on things you are weak at decreases self-confidence" (Pillay, 2014, para. 27). For things you are really bad at, you're only going to improve marginally. Perhaps this marginal improvement is extremely necessary and worth doing. Maybe you go from cooking ramen and grilled cheese sandwiches to cooking chicken and steak. It's unlikely you will ever compete with Gordon Ramsey in the kitchen, but knowing how to cook basic foods (even if it is a struggle to get there) is a tremendous improvement overeating impoverished student food. For one thing, you would be able to cook for a woman.

I mentioned I can fix motorcycles. I'm not bad; if I worked a little harder, I could be a competent motor-cycle mechanic. If I worked hard my whole life, would I be in the top two percent of mechanics for Harley-Davidson in the world? This is unlikely, but I would be good. If I worked on painting my whole life, I would not touch Piccaso's skill when he was a teenager. Also, I can shoot hoops, but I'm not going to try out for the NBA. Part of being a self-confident man is being realis-tic, as I mentioned. Your skills and goals should reflect more on who you are than who you want to be (though your self-concept, as I mentioned in the Introduction, is very important to your identity).

Michelle Mandel (2022, para. 5) attests that "we cause our own suffering." We make mistakes and grow from them. As Mandel (2022, para. 5) states, "An atmosphere of growth is integral to happiness." In this view, "Mis-takes are true growth opportunities," and I wager you to find a way we grow that does not involve, in some way or another, making a mistake (Mandel, 2022).

An advocate of mindfulness, like myself, may get carried away in recommending that you live in the moment. As Mandel (2022, para. 7) puts it, "We are very much our past," and we find continuity in the present with the decisions we have made, including our mistakes. For this reason, "You are wiser today than yesterday," states Mandel (2022, para. 13). Martin Heidegger was a proponent of mindfulness and possibly the first Western thinker to introduce the concept of mindfulness to a Western audience (through the influence of Taoism on his thought)—a fact that is very rarely acknowledged. Heidegger theorizes that the world is composed of Care, which is a way of stating that what is important to Being [*Dasein*] is the interactivity between beings (the words Heidegger employs are *neologisms* in the German language). As Johannes Lotz (2022, para. 1) puts it, "Every thing and every man is a being, as that which is; but [B]eing is the ground by which all beings are or a being is." That is to say: we have a relationship to others that is primordial; our dependence on people existed before we were born. We cannot be ourselves without other people, most literally our parents, but also our ancestors and the people around us. This realization causes us anxiety because we believe we are free individuals.

For Heidgger, the solution to anxiety is to focus your attention on Care (the things around you), such as the book you are reading, the nail you are hammering, the person you are speaking to, the meal you are eating, and so forth. Thinking, for Heidegger, is a reflexive reaction to an ongoing situation, a kind of "disruption" in the continuity that makes life simple and easy. Heidegger's philosophy is powerful, and in some ways helpful, though he struggled with the "continuity" of our pasts that Mandel advocates for as part of our identity. Heidegger joined the Nazi party in his native Germany in part because of his opposition to "thinking." Heidegger spent the last part of his life apologizing for this mistake, but his reputation was forever tainted. In Mandel's words, Heidegger was very much his past, even when he advocated for living in the present. I do yoga and meditate. I would be lying to you if I say I will ever forget my worst mistakes, even through this practice. On a song titled "Intern," Angel Olsen (2016) sings, "It doesn't matter who you are or what you've done / You've still got to wake up and be someone." This is the approach I take to the Care in my world, even if I can't forget my past mistakes. I doubt yours are as bad as mine. Maybe they are, but I doubt they are worse than Heidegger's.

Mandel (2022) rightly states that if you "accept where you are—you will suffer less." This truth does not mean we should stop dreaming or aiming for our goals (e.g. aiming for the moon to land on the Sears Tower), but it means our goals need to be realistic and achievable. Self-esteem (and, therefore, self-confidence) is enhanced when you meet your goals. You're smart, but are your *goals* SMART?

Specific

Measurable

Achievable

Realistic

Time-based

Sarah Kristenson offers some advice about what kind of goals to choose. She writes, "I want to be more confident is not a good goal" (Kristenson, 2022). The following, according to Kristenson, are realistic and effective goals to build self-confidence:

- Improve eye contact with people when speaking.
- Develop active listening skills.
- Refine your posture.
- Limit filler words (e.g. umm, uhh, and like) when speaking.
- Rehearse public speaking.
- Speak up more often.
- Expand your social network.
- Enhance your time management skills.

Maybe I put the cart before the horse. Maybe you have a hard time seeing value in yourself and are lower in the dumps than I thought. Maybe you're like me and have trouble getting out of bed and showering. Making goals, even to look people in the eye, can seem like a daunting task. In the next chapter, I will talk about finding self-love and using positive self-talk to build a foundation for a self-confident man who is not only satisfied in his situation but thrives and is actively looking for new opportunities in life.

UNLOCKING YOUR TRUE POTENTIAL WITH SELF-LOVE AND POSITIVE SELF-TALK

If you are at all like me, perhaps you have woken up on a given morning absolutely terrified people will find out your "secret." If you are very much like me, you may have woken up every morning nervous about the same thing. What was my "secret"? I had come from money, and I had lost it all. I made a series of bad investments. I had to learn how to live independently from nothing after that, and this is what taught me resilience and self-confidence. Yet, I was nervous I would be found out for my past. That people would know I had squandered so much in life (only to build it back from scratch). What is your "secret"?

If you feel like you're an imposter who doesn't truly deserve love, success, or respect, then you're not alone. In fact, there is a disorder colloquially known as "imposter syndrome" that describes precisely this feeling. An individual with low self-confidence believes it's only a matter of time before they're "found out" and abandoned by the people they care about. Imagine living life on edge like this (perhaps you don't need to imagine it). I had gone from steak dinners to sardines, and I rejected the opportunity to meet friends and go on dates because I was low on money. *All my fault*, I thought (even though I was scammed from some of it).

Self-love does not sound like a particularly masculine activity, at least from an initial assessment. Jackson Bliss (2014, para. 1) remarks that "self-love...sounds either like a euphemism for masturbation, a pretext for narcissism, or a prelude to egomania." In fact, it is none of the above. So far, you have followed me down Frost's road and made it partway through the forest. You expected bears and wolves; mountains and valleys; waterfalls and mermaids. You're getting a lecture on self-love instead. What's going on?

The fact is no one is confident in themselves all of the time. Those people who project perpetual confidence are often arrogant. In reality, self-confidence is a silent display of skill, attention to circumstances, and sensitivity to others. Being a man is about living life skillfully, in the words of John Gray. If you think of yourself as an iceberg, a self-confident man holds the majority of his self-love (i.e. ice) underwater. Marcus Aurelius, the Roman emperor, wrote his *Meditations* in part to share his wisdom with others, but also to learn the wisdom himself. Aurelius (2011) struggled with self-doubt over his life, especially during his tenure managing a vast empire, and he realized, "Our life is what our thoughts make it." Foreshadowing CBT by about 1,500 years, Aurelius declares, "You have power over your mind—not outside events. Realize this, and you will find strength" ("Marcus Aurelius quotes," 2022). If a Roman emperor needed to remind himself to have self-love, then you can probably put this lesson to work too.

Self-love does not mean thinking positively all the time. In fact, no one is able to do this without going insane. We need negative experiences to make positive ones meaningful and favorable. No one is asking you to artificially inflate yourself, but instead to simply have "an appreciation of one's own worth or virtue" (Merriam-Webster, n.d.). This is literally the textbook definition of self-love from Merriam-Webster.

If you are still cringing at the concept of "self-love," it is possibly because of social stigma that makes men think we are invincible. Society expects us to be completely objective when it comes to our emotions and self-esteem. However, no one can be totally objective about their circumstances. Moreover, we seem to have a hard time prioritizing ourselves over others—possibly because of the social responsibility we feel for others as men. *Self-care* is an act of self-love, wherein you value yourself enough to prioritize your happiness without sacrificing this happiness to please others. I will talk about this point more in the next chapter.

It is more acceptable for men to discuss our achievements than our feelings. Our achievements are worth discussing, but this state of affairs has to change to encompass our feelings as well. Too many men are angry, bitter, and cynical toward life; they see, as I stated in the Introduction, other men "succeed" and themselves "fail." I already mentioned that you do not know the successful men's struggles. I will now state that our accomplishments are contingent on our feelings and capacity for self-love.

A writer at *Medium* describes self-love as "being in a relationship with yourself" and insists that "you wouldn't tell your friend that they're ugly, stupid, or unlovable, would you?" ("Self-love for men," 2020, para. 1).

I have had this conversation with many men who are struggling with low self-confidence; they seem to think that they are subject to a separate set of standards than everyone else. They are the only person—or at least only man—who doesn't deserve forgiveness and grace. "What makes you so special?" I ask these men. Philosophically, we have a hard time projecting our first-person perspective to anyone else because we are the only creatures we know that have the lived experience of "I." Proving the existence of other people in this context is nontrivial and is often done by analogy. In many ways, human beings are a product of their community, most literally our families, but also our friends and neighbors. Having greater self-love means having a greater love for others. Unfortunately, for those men who have been put down all their lives (I know many), self-love seems like a distant dream. Sometimes, self-love comes from the "outside in," so it is important to hear words of affirmation to truly love ourselves and others.

Young boys are not shown much guidance and affection from other men. Perhaps you think showing love is for women. This stigma is a relatively recent development. Another Roman emperor, Cicero (1923), declares, "With the exception of wisdom, I'm inclined to believe the immortal gods have given nothing better to humanity than friendship." Friendships among men (that also function as mentorships) have had an important role in history. Perhaps you think emotions are for weaklings. Even the stoic philosophers who abstained from showing much emotion recognized that emotions are part of life. In fact, emotions are a part of all healthy beings, and we need emotions just like we need intellect or a healthy body.

As the writer at *Medium* ("Self-love for men," 2020, para. 7) puts it, "Thinking you're great is not the same thing as thinking others are below you." I hope you're ready to take the step into self-love, even though that may be the scariest part of the forest of all.

In our current media environment, women are constantly bombarded with messages of self-love, empowerment, and beauty. By contrast, men are not taught to accept mistakes and accept ourselves for making them. You have made mistakes like anybody else and can learn from them. Errors don't define you, and they don't make you undeserving of love. Andy Warhol refused to be photographed with a pimple because he knew it was a temporary blemish on what he perceived to be a relatively eternal beauty. Can you recognize that there is a man behind the pimple, even if he happens to be photographed with it?

Self-love is crucial for men because we need to love ourselves before we are able to love others, such as our partners and friends. As such, "Self-love is not only for yourself. You can't pour from an empty cup. If you don't love yourself, you'll struggle to love others the way you both deserve" ("Self-love for men," 2020, para. 12).

Andrew Ferebee (2022, para. 7) describes self-love as the "routine maintenance of a high power machine that is you." Ferebee (2022, para. 25) adds, "Without self-love, even the strongest of men would simply burn out and crash within a matter of months." Ferebee offers some tips for men to practice self-love and self-care in our daily lives (recall that self-care is a practice of self-love):

- *Create an open space and learn to decompress.* Do what you want to do for your self-care, within limits. Approach every day as a gift. Every day is a perfect day to wake up, breathe in the air, and stand in the sun. Diogenes of Synope, a philosopher who lived in a barrel in what is now modern-day Turkey, famously savored his time in the sun, so much so that he asked a visiting Alexander the Great to get out of his way when Alexander cast a shadow accidentally blocking it.
- *Forgo mindless consumption and get creative instead!* For the majority of our time on this earth, men created rather than consumed. Ask yourself: when was the last time you created something because you wanted to do it, rather

than because you were paid for it? Access that creative energy inside of you; it beats passively enjoying the products of others.

- *Celebrate the small victories, or you'll miss them all.* Human beings have a tendency to exaggerate the negatives and downplay the positives in our lives. We evolved this way, so this feature is perfectly understandable; the cost of a mistake for a paleolithic man may have been his life, whereas for us the cost of a mistake is a broken Excel formula. We cannot limit our celebrations to big things because they happen so rarely. Treat yourself. Did you submit your project on time? That is a (small) victory.

- *Create a morning routine to calibrate your mind.* There are a lot of sayings about this: "early to bed, early to rise makes a man healthy and wise," "the early bird gets the worm," and so forth. There is something to be said about early risers; you plan out your day when everyone else is still asleep. You can do yoga. You can see the city or the countryside when it is silent. For me, 5 a.m. is the perfect time to meditate, do cardio, or listen to a podcast. The first thing I *don't* do in the morning is check my email, the news, or social media.

- *Own your boundaries in relationships.* As Ferebee (2022, para. 78) puts it, "Unseen fences are useless." We cannot guess what people expect of us, and we cannot keep people guessing about what we expect either. We have to talk openly about what we want and expect in our relationships. Aristotle makes a case that lying is acceptable under certain circumstances. Immanuel Kant challenges this claim and says it is never acceptable to lie. Kant provides an example for his position; say a robber is at your door looking for your friend. You know exactly where your friend is (in your house). Do you tell the robber? I, of course, would not, but Kant offers a hypothetical alternative; the robber goes into your house anyway, incensed that you lied, whereas if you told him the truth, perhaps he would have turned around. The truth and honesty have a therapeutic effect on people, to say nothing about how they nurture our soul.
- *Meditate.* I talked about the importance of mindfulness in the last chapter. Meditation is one way to "jump-start" the practice of mindfulness, but it is not a walk in the park to start meditating either. I know many men who can't sit alone with their thoughts for 30 seconds, but I also know many men who can

touch their toes. Try stretching—namely yoga—if you cannot concentrate on meditation. Since yoga is a mind-body exercise, it will force your brain to calm down as it also lowers your breath and soothes your muscles.

- *Have you-time (for introverts).* Some of us like being left alone with our thoughts and ideas. Extroverts, of course, find this appalling, but introverts do not get refreshed from a 300-person rager. You know what's best for you; whether you are an introvert or extrovert, ensure that you use your you-time for creation rather than consumption, per my second tip.
- *Hang out with awesome people (for extroverts).* Contrary to popular belief, "chatting online is not proper social interaction" (Ferebee, 2022, para. 99). Ferebee recommends you invite people out to real-world events. "It takes leadership, effort, and creativity to bring people together," writes Ferebee (2022, para. 101). Thus, making this happen is no easy task. However, we all need human connections (including introverts), so facilitating interaction with others is crucial to self-care.
- *Establish meaningful relationships.* As the saying goes, "A shared joy is double joy; shared sorrow is half a sorrow" (Ferebee, 2022, para. 104).

Relationships are crucial to making life worth living, to say nothing about giving you self-confidence. You don't need many close friends, just some. As another saying goes, "When you die and you have five good friends, you've had a good life" (Ferebee, 2022, para. 106).

- *Have fun and laugh at life.* If you cannot laugh or have fun (right now), think about what made you come alive in your youth. Recall what that spark was and regain it. I guarantee you have not changed so much from that time.

- *Push boundaries.* "Self-love is masculine. Every man should do it," writes Ferebee (2022, para. 114). Men are trailblazers and visionaries; we have always pushed boundaries and created new things since time immemorial. Perhaps you can push the boundary that tells you it's unmasculine to care for yourself before you are genuinely able to care for others.

Rachel Eddins offers another perspective on how to pursue self-love and self-care for men. She states that these practices "tune out negativity" (Eddins, 2020, para. 2). A negative mindset takes a toll on your mental health. Furthermore, people will have opinions about you no matter what. You cannot control that. People have opinions on Joe DiMaggio, whether deep-dish pizza is pizza, what color a dress is in an optical illusion, and so forth. Letting go of things that you have no control over is one sure way to boost self-confidence and improve self-care: then, you have the bandwidth to actually affect the things you do have control over.

Like Ferebee, Eddins recommends you celebrate your accomplishments. "Never be afraid to have a toast to what serves your ultimate happiness," she writes (Eddins, 2020, para. 7). Part of the way we can toast to ourselves every day is to practice positive *self-talk*. Self-talk is what it sounds like; it is how you talk to yourself. Maybe it's your inner monologue. Maybe it's how you think. If you're at all like I was, your inner monologue might be extremely negative. For instance, you may be replaying upsetting thoughts and events over and over in your head and tearing yourself down for them. Let's try to change that.

Kimberly Holland argues that our self-talk is influenced by unconscious processes and reveals itself in our thoughts, beliefs, the questions we ask, and the ideas or ideals we hold. That is, if we practice negative self-talk, we are likely to be negative in disposition. Our lives may be even more negative. The exact opposite is true with positive self-talk. In fact, positive self-talk is likely to provide you with health benefits, such as the following:

- increased vitality
- greater life satisfaction
- improved immune function
- reduced pain
- better cardiovascular health
- better physical well-being
- reduced risk for death
- less stress and distress

Negative self-talk takes a few forms, which I have outlined below:

- *Personalization*: Here, you blame yourself for everything that goes wrong. You think you're responsible for the actions of others and that their actions are the result of you rather than a million other factors in another person's life. We all have problems that we're going through. Most people are too focused on their own problems to notice yours.
- *Magnifying*: Here, you focus on negative aspects of a situation and ignore any and all positive aspects. I already spoke about how this kind of cognitive bias is an evolutionary adaptation. The fact that it is evolutionary does not mean it cannot be practically changed, however. Try to think about your negative responses as being a

"natural" mechanism that just needs to be regulated a little bit.

- *Catastrophizing*: Here, you expect the worst and rarely let logic or reason persuade you otherwise. I have no idea how many times I have catastrophized over the course of my life. I thought average situations in public would lead to my death or dissolution. I thought a failure at work meant a failure at life. I thought because I was rejected by one date meant I would never go on a date ever again. Catastrophizing is challenging to avoid (without consciously stopping it entirely) because it is not empirical; even though catastrophe never struck, I was always sure that it would.

- *Polarizing*: Also called zero-sum thinking, here, you believe that the world is black and white or good and bad; there is no middle ground. As I already stated, most of our life experiences will be in the middle ground. There will be very few things in life that are purely good or purely bad, and if they are (either one), I think you will know immediately.

Negative thinking can be turned into positive, or at least neutral, thinking fairly easily. Compare the following statements:

Negative: I'll disappoint everyone because I changed my mind about X. Everyone thought I was deeply committed to X.

Positive: I have the power to change my mind. Others will understand. Maybe X wasn't such a great idea.

Negative: I failed today and embarrassed myself in front of everyone.

Positive: At least I tried! That alone took courage.

Negative: I'm overweight and out of shape. Better just give up now!

Positive: I am capable and strong. I can go to the gym. I want to get healthier.

Negative: I've never done this before. Watch me be bad at it!

Positive: This is a wonderful opportunity to learn something new and grow as a person.

Negative: There's no way this will work!

Positive: I can and will give it my best shot to make it work!

Simple enough, right? I'm not asking you to change your situation (yet), only your perspective. Changing negative thinking to positive (or neutral) thinking takes practice. In this chapter, I will describe some approaches to help you improve your self-talk. For now, though, here are some consequences of negative self-talk from Elizabeth Scott. Like there are benefits to positive-self talk—in fact, positive self-talk is a strong predictor of success—there are downsides to continuing the spiral of negativity you may be stuck in.

Negative self-talk leads to

- *Limited thinking*: The more you tell yourself you can't do something, the more you believe it. Soon, you may not leave your house due to shrinking world syndrome (SWS). Negative self-talk limits the potential you have for action and experiencing self-actualization in the world, and it sets up a self-fulfilling prophecy.
- *Perfectionism*: Here, you determine that "great isn't as good as perfect." (Scott, 2022, para. 10) Scott points out that perfectionism tends to be associated with high achievement, as high-achieving projects tend to involve more stress. Scott (2022) states that "mere high achievers tend to do better than perfectionistic counterparts," because perfectionism is a cognitive bias that results in inefficiency, whereas simply working hard is not.
- *Depression*: Negative self-talk exacerbates depressive symptoms and, if left untreated, can manifest as clinical depression.

- *Relationship challenges*: Negative self-talk may facilitate a lack of communication between yourself and other people. Perhaps you worry that you're not good enough to be taken seriously (see impostor syndrome later). Here, simple criticism (even if it is joking) can take its toll on you. If you are surrounded by negative self-talk, hearing it from another can be devastating.

Now that you know what negative self-talk is, how do you stop it? Scott provides some tips:

- *Catch your critic.* Your inner critic says things to you that you would never say to anyone else. Realize that and "catch your critic" when he arrives (Scott, 2022, para. 18). You should learn how to differentiate between your critic and you.
- *Recall that thoughts and feelings aren't the same.* Just because you're thinking something does not mean it's true, nor does it mean that it's a part of you as a feeling. If I say, "I'm the worst person in the world," this is not a true statement. It's also not a feeling because the feeling is that I just feel bad (which has nothing to do with how "bad" I am). Treat a thought like

a leaf that flows through the wind or a blemish on your hand. You can choose to look at it or not.

- *Nickname your critic.* Related to my first tip, give your critic a funny nickname. "Sweet, Doomer Andrew is here. I can't wait to hear how bad I am. Where's Party Andrew or Making Money Andrew?" Giving your critic a funny name may illustrate that your inner critic is a force outside of you, and you don't have to listen to him.

- *Contain your negativity.* Limit your negative thinking to only certain things or a certain part of the day. I admit, I think negatively when I wake up in the morning. It lasts maybe 10 minutes. I don't want to get up or start the day. Then, I find *one* thing I am looking forward to and build the rest of the day from that.

- *Change negativity to neutrality.* If you can't be positive, be neutral. Maybe it's not a great learning opportunity to try something new. However, you have to do it anyway, so you may as well do it.

- *Cross-examine your inner critic.* Imagine you are in a courtroom, and your inner critic is perjuring himself by making up lies about you. You hired a competent defense attorney (yourself); you want to cross-examine your negative thoughts and see how they really hold up. Spoiler alert: they probably don't hold up in a court of law.

- *Think like a friend.* I stated earlier that self-love is like being in a friendship with yourself. Treat yourself like a friend and not like your worst enemy. Do you tell your friends they're worthless or good-for-nothing? No, so why do you tell yourself that?

- *Change your perspective.* Ask yourself: is what you're upset about going to matter in five days, five months, or five years? I will go out on a limb here and state that anything that won't matter in five years probably doesn't matter now.

- *Say your thoughts aloud.* This may seem paradoxical, but stating your negative thoughts aloud takes away some of their power. Perhaps you will realize how unreasonable and unrealistic your thoughts are when you actually hear them.

- *Stop the thought.* Tell yourself, "No, not today. I'm too tired. Let me take a nap, and Doomer Andrew can get back to me later if he wants."

- *Replace the bad with some good.* This is a subtle suggestion as most situations are not strictly good or bad. Recall the good elements that accompanied the bad when a so-called "bad" memory pops up. Yes, I went on an awful date the other day, but the chicken parmesan was amazing.

- *Avoid absolutes.* You are not the judge of the universe, so you cannot make declarative statements about yourself or others as if you are. There is always nuance to every perspective. No one is undeserving of love. No one is "not good enough."

Perhaps your low self-confidence manifests as *imposter syndrome.* A psychologist writing for the Cleveland Clinic defines imposter syndrome as an "overwhelming feeling that you don't deserve success" ("Imposter syndrome: What...," 2022). Perhaps you are "pretending to be an adult who's capable of buying a home or raising another human" ("Imposter syndrome: What...," 2022, para. 1). Maybe you have no idea how you got your job, and you're surprised you still have it. I've been there.

Imposter syndrome can turn into a thought cycle with serious negative consequences. According to this writer, seven in ten adults experienced imposter syndrome at one point or another ("Imposter syndrome: What...," 2022). Symptoms of impostor syndrome include

- crediting luck or other reasons for your success
- being afraid of being seen as a failure
- overworking being seen as the only way to meet expectations
- feeling unworthy of attention or affection
- downplaying accomplishments
- holding back from reaching attainable goals

The first step to overcoming imposter syndrome is acknowledging it. Then, the same steps to build self-confidence can be followed. For instance, if you have measured and reasonable successes at work, it's hard to feel like an imposter.

Imposter syndrome, like low-self confidence in general, may lead you to avoid responsibility out of fear. You will miss out on a lot, as you probably know from experience. Fans of the Smiths may recall Morrissey's (1987) lyric, "Shyness is nice / Shyness can stop you / From doing the things in life you want to." In this chapter, I hope you learned that self-love and self-care are not just for crybabies; self-love and self-care are crucial to making a man who can stand up for himself, his family, and his community. Men take risks. You cannot succeed in life without risks. I know you are willing to take a risk because you are reading this book. You believe there is a chance—a strong one, in fact—that you can build self-confidence and become a new man.

In Nietzsche's (1974) terms, you can "become who you are."

In this chapter, I spoke about how to shower yourself with kindness—how to be a friend to yourself, instead of your own worst enemy. We are deep into the forest now, so we settle in a clearing and eat lunch. Other travelers from the mountains join us. How do you assert your needs in the eyes of other people? How do you live life on your own terms? Follow me into the next chapter to find out.

4

LEARNING TO LIVE LIFE ON YOUR OWN TERMS

In the last chapter, I described how to challenge imposter syndrome and anxiety using self-love and positive self-talk. In this chapter, I will discuss another sign of a man with low self-confidence: a people-pleaser. By the end of this chapter, you will know how to establish healthy boundaries and avoid people-pleasing like you avoid imposter syndrome and anxiety. Let's get started.

Ask yourself if you struggle to set and maintain boundaries. Do you have trouble saying "no" to requests you don't want to do? If so, you may be a people-pleaser. People-pleasers do what it takes to make other people happy. In principle, this is not a bad thing because most people appreciate this kind of attention. However, people-pleasing can undermine your personal progress and potential if you don't put yourself first. For instance, a people-pleaser may believe they're not deserving of the space, time, and attention they provide for others. Moreover, some people will see this attitude and exploit the people-pleaser. Setting healthy boundaries is a primary way to avoid people-pleasing, while still being a good person to others.

Kendra Cherry (2021a, para. 1) remarks that "going too far to please others can leave you emotionally depleted, stressed, and anxious." People-pleasers are highly attuned to others, and superficially, they may be seen as agreeable, helpful, and kind. Maybe they practice sociography, wherein pleasing others is a means to maintain relationships with them. The initial reaction you get as a people-pleaser is not worth the long-term consequences of putting others before yourself to the point of your detriment.

There are a number of signs you may be a people-pleaser:

- You have difficulty saying "no" (especially for things you don't want to do).
- You are preoccupied with what others might think.
- You feel guilty when you tell people "no."

- You fear that turning people down will make them think you are mean or selfish.
- You struggle with feelings of low self-esteem.
- You do things for people to get them to love you.
- You're always telling people you're sorry.
- You take blame, even if it's not your fault.
- You don't have free time because you are always doing things for other people.
- You neglect your own needs.
- You pretend to agree with people when you don't.

Cherry (2021a, para. 7) remarks that while people-pleasers are viewed as "generally empathetic, thoughtful, and caring," this is actually hiding a poor self-image, a need to take control, and overachievement. I suffered from people-pleasing too. I noticed early on in life that people would like me more if I did them favors or helped them out. I thought this was a good way to build social capital; I didn't realize that when I needed help, these people were not there to "please" me back. I had spread myself too thin trying to make friends and allies. When it was time for my needs, there was no energy left, and my "friends" were self-pleasers. I realized that if I didn't have these superficial relationships, I would have more time for myself and more time to nurture real relationships and friendships. There are a number of additional symptoms to people-pleasing and strategies to address them, but first, I'd like to talk about the causes of people-pleasing.

- *Poor self-esteem*: You are reading this book to increase your self-esteem and self-confidence. A people-pleaser does not value their own desires and needs. A people-pleaser requires external validation.
- *Insecurity*: A people-pleaser bases their identity on the needs and preferences of others. The end result of this attitude is insecurity. You are unlikely to discover who you are if you only live for others.
- *Perfectionism*: Perfectionism is a sign of low self-esteem and low self-confidence stemming from your need to hold yourself to a standard you would not hold others to. I worked years and years on several of my books. I have met other writers who finished their novel in three months. They are not perfectionists. Are their novels good? Of course, they are.
- *Past experiences*: You may have painful, difficult, or traumatic past experiences. Perhaps you suffered abuse and try to please people in order to avoid the triggers responsible for this abuse.

I mentioned some signs of people-pleasing already. Here are symptoms that emerge when you pursue this line of behavior:

- *Anger and frustration*: You do things reluctantly or out of obligation. There is a cycle that takes place; you help someone, feel mad at them for taking advantage of you, and feel regret for even trying to help.
- *Anxiety and stress*: As a people-pleaser, you stretch your own physical and mental resources too thin. Of course, helping other people can have mental health benefits too. However, if all you do is help people, you might end up experiencing the negative consequences of excess stress, both yours and theirs.
- *Depleted willpower*: Our willpower is a finite resource, like oil. We are less likely to have resolve and willpower if we're people-pleasing. We need to save some energy for ourselves if we want to have a self-actualized life.
- *Lack of authenticity*: Being a people-pleaser means you obscure your authentic self. Jean-Paul Sartre uses the example of a waiter; if your role is reactive, you are unable to assert yourself. Waiters, given this limitation (and their frustration), will express themselves by

appearing lazy or cynical. This is the only form of authenticity when your potential for self-expression is limited. To become a self-actualized person, you have to care for others as well as yourself.

- *Weaker relationships*: Your relationships are not strong when you are a people-pleaser. Your "friends" may take your kindness and attentiveness for granted and exploit you. In fact, they may exploit you without even realizing they are doing so; this is simply the image you have projected to the world that they are reacting to.

If you are a people-pleaser, it's not too late to stop being one. Below are tips to challenge your people-pleasing and build your self-confidence:

- *Establish boundaries.* I will talk about boundaries in detail a little later in the chapter. For now, communicate your limits to the people around you. Teach people around you to understand your limits, if you must. For instance, take calls only when you are able to. Have control over what you're going to do and when you're going to do it.

- *Start small.* Assert yourself in small ways first; say "no" to smaller requests, for instance. Express your opinion about something small.
- *Set goals and priorities.* Consider the whole you: what do you want to spend your time on? When do you want to do it? Who do you want to help? These questions should come before you agree to take on the tasks and burdens of others.
- *Stall for time.* This is my favorite tip. When someone asks you for a favor, tell them you need time to think about it. Before you give them a response, ask yourself the following:

1. How much time will this take?
2. Is this something I really want to do?
3. Do I have time to do it?
4. How stressed am I gonna be in if I say "yes"?

Research displays that taking even a short pause before making a decision improves the quality of your decision-making abilities.

- *Assess the request.* Look for signs that people are trying to take advantage of your generosity. It's possible these people will be "unavailable" to return the favor when the karmic reciprocity is requested. Cat Stevens sings about friends like this when he says, "I know many fine feathered friends / But their friendliness depends on how you do / They know many sure-fired ways / To find out the one who pays / And how you do" (Georgiou, 1970).

- *Avoid making excuses.* Be direct when you say "no" to people. Remember that "no" is a complete sentence. Do not give them contextual information about why you said "no" because, otherwise, they may try to poke a hole in your objection. When George Costanza in *Seinfeld* didn't want to do volunteer work, he ended up weaving an excuse that involved him having to go to Paris in order to have an alibi. As Sir William Scott declares, "Oh! What a tangled web we weave / When we practice to deceive" (Robertson, 2003).

- *Relationships require give and take.* Certain degrees of reciprocity are required in relationships of any kind. When you please someone, they ought to take steps to please you in return, even if it's not immediately after or in the same way. A legitimate friendship is among the most precious gifts on this planet, to say nothing of a romantic relationship. It's up to

your friend and partner to nurture the
relationship, not just you.

- *Help out when you want to help.* Don't give up
  being kind and thoughtful, but be firm and
  steadfast. Contribute to strong, lasting
  relationships and projects you are interested in.
  Examine your motivations and intentions.
  Don't do things because you fear rejection and
  crave approval.

Keep doing good things, but on your own terms. Kindness doesn't deserve rewards, but you may get some rewards if you find other kind people.

An effective way to quit people-pleasing is to switch your terms from "I don't" to "I can't." When you can't do something, it's simply impossible. Keep "I can't" and "impossible" as synonyms in your mind.

There are a few more tips to stop people-pleasing before I move on to boundaries more generally. They are mentioned below:

- *Understand your self-worth.* We people-please
  because we undervalue our worth. Has anyone
  ever "people-pleased" you? Unnatural, isn't it? I
  think it's only due to our low-confidence
  cognitive distortion that we believe that we are

the only people who are not worthy of attention.

- *You'll never please everyone.* Check out *Jane Eyre* or Shakespeare reviews on Amazon. Some people don't even like the classics of literature.
- *It's impossible to control what other people think or feel.* Let go.
- *Speak up for yourself.* Stand up for what you believe in, to a point (don't get yourself into hot water). Most people, men and women, find men with conviction to be powerful and admirable. Whether you're attracting a mate or succeeding in work, you have to speak up.
- *Know that self-care is not selfish.* It's necessary. Practice self-care so that your people-pleasing doesn't lead to a full-blown crisis.
- *Make room for you.* Remember that you should be your first or second priority (depending on whether you have a partner or children). Maybe your child should be your first priority, but Jenny from HR is not at the top of the list. You don't have to do what she says just because she asks politely.

For the remainder of the chapter, I will describe how to establish boundaries, which are healthy rules for human relationships. The benefits of establishing boundaries is that they improve relationships and self-esteem and allow you to conserve energy.

Having boundaries is what allows us to grow and be vulnerable. Critically, boundaries are not unyielding and can be flexible.

Jennifer Chesak (2018, para. 4) defines a boundary as a "sense of agency over one's physical space, body, and feelings." Chesak (2018, para. 5) adds that boundaries are "connecting points since they provide healthy rules for navigating relationships, intimate or professional." As Melissa Coats (Chesak, 2018, para. 6) puts it, "Boundaries protect relationships from becoming unsafe." Boundaries make *you* the priority.

There are boundaries we do not cross. This mostly has to do with harming another person. Beyond this very important exception, however, it's not necessary to "draw your boundaries in permanent ink" (Chesak, 2018, para. 7). I think you will find that your values can be steadfast but also flexible to the situation at hand.

The reason you should establish and maintain boundaries is because you can resent yourself if you don't advocate for yourself first. Boundaries allow us to have different reactions depending on the situation, while maintaining the energy to care for ourselves. For this reason, "I" statements set boundaries, and "can" or "can't" statements do too.

An example of crossing a boundary is oversharing. Oversharing is a way to keep someone emotionally hostage. Oversharing makes you involved in someone else's life to an inappropriate degree, as you did not choose it for yourself. Perhaps you have been on the receiving end of this emotional manipulation, or you did not realize boundaries were crossed when you were conversing with someone. Check out the list of cues below to determine if someone's boundaries are being crossed:

- They want more space.
- They avoid eye contact.
- They turn away or look sideways.
- They back up.
- Their conversational response is limited to words or phrases.
- Excessive nodding or use of "uh-huh" on their part.
- Their voice becomes high-pitched.
- They perform nervous gestures like laughing, talking fast, or talking with their hands.
- They fold their arms or stiffen their posture.
- They flinch.
- They wince.

If you don't know, just ask! Ask about peoples' boundaries, so everyone is on the same page. If asking is not feasible for some reason, trust your instincts. Your sense of boundaries depends on how you grew up. Maybe the home life for you wasn't the best, so your sense of boundaries is warped. I still think we can be a good judge of character, even if we have insufficiently developed boundaries. Be extremely cautious that the people that appear to be exploiting you in life are doing just that and not something else.

Michelle Brooten-Brooks (2022, para. 1) defines boundaries as "fences" between humans, similar to fences between homes or lands. Boundaries are the "physical and emotional limits of appropriate behavior" (Brooten-Brooks, 2022). Of boundaries, Brooten-Brooks outlines three types: clear, rigid, and open.

Healthy boundaries involve the communication of wants and needs and the respect of the wants and needs of others. Abuse (physical, sexual, or emotional) is perhaps the clearest example of a violation of boundaries.

Are you concerned that you have open boundaries instead of ones that are rigid or clear? Below are five ways to set boundaries and make them firmer:

- *Enjoy self-reflection.* Be the detective of your own psyche. Explore what's happening to you. Try journaling. In thinking about what makes you happy, you may recognize what is anathema to your comfort and happiness as well.
- *Start small.* Set boundaries at a comfortable pace. Set boundaries regarding small items first before moving on to greater ones. Regarding speaking up, I already mentioned that you can "start small" in voicing your opinion too.
- *Set boundaries early.* Let everyone know what your boundaries are. So long as people know where you stand, there is less potential for confusion and boundary crossing.
- *Be consistent.* Don't change your boundaries from day-to-day! Firm boundaries that are consistent across time will not make people think you are malleable or exploitable.
- *Talk, talk, talk!* See the example below.

Let's say Jenny from HR wants you to work on expense reports. She has been emailing you about it nonstop. Expense reports are not your purview, and Jenny is not your supervisor. You don't want to do the expense reports. How do you say "no"?

One way is to simply say "no"; you can say, "No, Jenny. I will not do the expense reports. Sorry." Another way is more diplomatic; you can buy some time by stating, "Hey Jenny, I can see you really want to reach me about these expense reports. I think you might be aware that I'm in Communications and not accounting. However, if you think I could be of use here, can you let me know a time we can meet about these reports and talk more?" Perhaps Jenny assumes you are a math-wiz when you're not. Talking helps establish and clarify boundaries. The worst things to do are complete the reports (and become resentful) and state that you can't do it, rather than you won't.

"Why not?" Jenny may ask. "Why can't you do it?" It's best to not even go down that path of explanation.

I made the case in this book, though not explicitly, that we are dependent on others for our identity and sense of self. No man is an island. It is from this perspective that we should put ourselves first. The level to which society is important to our identity may motivate us to sublimate ourselves to the needs of others. This is an absolutely bad approach, especially for men.

Having good boundaries teaches you to be your own champion. Boundaries allow you to show yourself love because you reject your boundaries being crossed just because other people want something. A self-confident man cares for his family and the people around him, but a man cannot care for a partner, child, or community if he does not know who he is or lacks a sense of self.

Another way to put the lesson in this chapter is: *don't think too hard*. Talk instead. You are evolutionarily primed to make judgements, and more often than not, these judgements are correct. I have been in situations where I thought, "This is bad, I shouldn't stay here," but I soldiered on just to see what happened (or to please others). The results were not good. Listen to your gut when it screams out at you to leave, to stay with someone, to trust someone or not. Your body is sensitive to what is good for you, and so is your mind. You are reading this book not to find out something new, but to tell you what you *already* know. That is the wager of Socrates and the past 2,000 years of Western philosophy. Your task is to put what you know into practice, to emerge at the end of Frost's road as a self-confident man who is his own person and a benefit to the community. I think if it was possible for me, it is possible for you.

In the next chapter I will talk about developing a healthy mindset, but first, I want to talk a bit more about establishing boundaries in your personal life.

5

MASTERING YOUR MINDSET

Having boundaries is about respecting yourself and others. You cannot respect others without respecting yourself. I remember I was dating a woman, Natalie, who invited me to meet her parents for Easter. This was a big step. I did all the regular things: met Natalie's mom, met her dad, got a little drunk, played with three big dogs and two cats, and went to the local museum associated with the town.

Well, I have a vice. I think we all do. Mine are regional burger chains. I'm not talking about McDonalds and Burger King (which are fine), but rather In-and-Out, Jack in the Box, Five Guys, and the like. I just like to try them. It's not like I don't hit the gym afterwards or anything.

Anyway, this town had a regional burger place that was relatively famous. Let's say it rhymes with "Sheckers." I really wanted to try their burger. I informed Natalie, at the start of the trip, I'd like to go to Sheckers *if we have time.* That was a conditional statement because I knew that during Easter I would be eating honied ham and mashed potatoes. "If we had time" was the qualifying part of the statement.

Boy, did we have time. We had time to go to the local museum, to the park, to the library, to feed a goat, and so forth. We did everything except go to Sheckers.

I mentioned in the last chapter that you can't be a people-pleaser, or your needs get ignored or discarded. My needs are relatively simple, gosh darn it; all I want is a regional burger in the town that I'm in. I am not asking for the moon, but a realistic goal that can be built around previous obligations.

I'm not saying Natalie and I broke up over a Sheckers burger, but other issues were underlying that relationship. Namely, I vocalized my needs (remember to talk, talk, talk), but her needs took precedent. You should recall that a relationship is a cooperation, not a competition.

My mindset changed after my relationship with Natalie. Before I dated Natalie, I wouldn't have even voiced my desire for Sheckers. I would have just shut up and gone with the flow. I was a people-pleaser. I gained some confidence with Natalie, and I realized there were other women out there that I could voice my needs to and have them met. That's when I met Megan. Our third date was to a regional burger place. I made sure to have two formal, respectable dates before I subjected her to that.

A mindset is defined by Kendra Cherry (2021b, para. 2) as a "set of beliefs that shape how you make sense of the world." In philosophy (or at least, in German), a mindset is called a *Weltanschauung*, a worldview or way you make sense of facts. It includes beliefs about free will, morality, aesthetics, and other preferences. Likewise, a mindset or *Weltanschauung* influences how you think, feel, behave, and deal with challenges. My *Weltanschauung* includes a solid appreciation for regional burger chains and a committed belief that we can change who we are by altering our habits.

You may recall the Marcus Aurelius quote that introduces this book and is also found in Chapter 3. Aurelius predicts what will be demonstrated in this chapter empirically, that the mindset you adopt for yourself profoundly affects your life. If you view yourself as able to change and grow, you have a higher predictor of success compared to those who have a fixed mindset (other things remaining the same).

I'm getting a little ahead of myself here. Carol Dweck divides mindsets into types: growth and fixed. The table below illustrates differences in thought between the two mindsets.

Fixed Mindset	Growth Mindset
Either I'm good at it or I'm not.	I can learn to do anything I want.
That's just who I am. I can't change it.	I'm a constantly evolving work in progress.
If you have to work hard, you don't have the ability.	The more you challenge yourself, the smarter you become.
If I don't try, then I won't fail.	I only fail when I stop trying.
That job position is totally out of my league.	That job position looks challenging. Let me apply for it.

Jeremy Sutton (2021, para. 6) describes that "individuals who believe their talents can be developed through hard work, good strategies, and input from others have a 'growth' mindset." Alternatively, a fixed mindset considers such talents to be innate gifts that cannot be easily changed.

In reality, we are all a mixture of fixed and growth mindsets. A growth mindset is generally more conducive to personal growth, but not at all times. It is up to the self-confident man to know when circumstances of his life can be changed and when they are out of his control.

Those of us who believe, deep down, that people can change have a growth mindset. These people believe we can get smarter with the right opportunities, degrees of effort, and self-belief. I am one of those people.

A slight aside is warranted. I think about the way I grew up, and I struggled with math in part because my father scolded me for doing poorly on it. It occurs that "praising effort in children leads to a growth mindset while encouraging inherent ability leads to a fixed-ability framework" (Sutton, 2021, para. 18). If you want to instill a growth mindset in your children (which I assume you do), it is worth praising effort and creativity rather than innate abilities or outcomes. Perhaps I could have been a "math person" if I hadn't been taught that being bad at math was a moral failing.

Let's get back to becoming a more self-confident man. Sutton (2021, para. 16) writes that "adopting a growth mindset dramatically changes how you approach life and encourages success in education, business, and even relationships." We are confronted with daily dilemmas, some small and some relatively impactful (remember what James calls "genuine options"). For instance, say we didn't get into our dream school. How do we respond?

- They were never going to let me in.
- What can I do to keep up my goal? Maybe I should apply next year or contact them to see if anything else can be done.

The first bullet represents a fixed mindset and the second a growth one. Let's be frank; you may not be able to get into that school. However, you never know what connections you may make to help you in the future, even if you just inquire. Think about another scenario. A project doesn't go well at work. Do you say

- What can we learn here?
- I didn't have the skills to do it in the first place.

In this case the options are reversed. The first represents a growth mindset and the second a fixed one. In the words of Sutton (2021, para. 40), "A growth mindset puts you back in control."

Consider what rejection teaches you. I talked before about antifragility. This means you improve with each setback. Not every setback can even be viewed as such.

How often do you seek out people who think differently than you? If you have an open mind, you can aim to learn from people, instead of beating them in a debate. I know that if I am presented with new information, I alter my view or replace it, even if it encounters some opposition.

A growth mindset involves embracing the joy of being wrong. If we are mistaken, this is an opportunity to update our thinking. As Sutton (2021, para. 49) states, "Focus on improving [yourself] rather than proving [to others]."

I have a fondness for Sartre, but I'm not a true existentialist. They are too depressing. That being said, in the case of a growth mindset, it and existentialism line up; making mistakes and learning from them provide you with freedom. If you had no potential to fail, you would have no freedom.

Nick Wignall writes that all human beings have a gift, the capacity for learning. This means that we can all adopt a growth mindset. Let me put it another way; there are people who are really good at piano. They have a "talent" for it. I guarantee you I can find a so-called "talentless" guy and, with enough training, he may even excell the natural talent at piano. If you've read this far in this book, you may think I'm a good writer. Do I have natural talent? I have no idea. I worked on it so long I wouldn't even be able to tell the difference. A much better writer than me, Henry Miller, attests that he wrote hundreds of pages of garbage before he published his first book, *Tropic of Cancer*. Like I said, you should praise effort, not ability. You can do a lot with dedication. You can do a lot with a positive mindset.

Wignall (2019, para. 21) lets you in on a little secret: "People will always resent you for being willing to do what they aren't." If you're afraid to fail (or be alone), you will never self-actualize or achieve your potential. As Wignall (2019, para. 23) puts it, "A fixed mindset does not allow people the luxury of becoming. They have to already be."

So how do you "unfix" a fixed mindset? Cherry provides some clues:

- *Focus on the journey.* I can't tell you the amount of things I've learned on the way to a destination. What is a destination, as such? There is always further to go, so in essence, there is only a journey. As I stated before, a self-confident man savors the process of discovery as much as the discovery itself.

- *Incorporate "yet."* You haven't mastered a given task yet. There is still time to go, like there is further to go on the way to your "destination." You can overcome nearly anything with enough time and practice.
- *Pay attention to your words and thoughts.* Think positively (and realistically); practice mindfulness. Realize if and when your mind is lying to you. Realize that thoughts are not facts.
- *Take on challenges.* Don't be afraid to make mistakes. Don't be afraid to fail at math. Aim for something that will build resilience and perseverance. Develop antifragility.
- *View failure in a positive light.* What is failure if not a learned experience? I learned not to invest my money in shady dealings. I learned not to trust people that set off red flags. I learned to watch out for myself. These are life lessons that I wish I didn't have to go through, but that ultimately made me better off in the long run.
- *View challenges as opportunities for self-improvement.* There is no way to improve at something without trying and failing a little bit. The men that persevered across history—I am thinking Isaac Newton here—did not succumb to the first failed experiment. Napoleon did not give up after his first loss. You are in great

company if you have to try something a few
times to get it right.

- *Understand your own limitations.* I talked already
  about how I can't win a game of basketball
  against Michael Jordan, who is rapidly
  approaching the age where he is eligible for
  Medicare. I cannot climb a mountain (yet). I can
  pitch a tent but not blueprint a mansion. I bet I
  could do a lot of things if I put the time and
  effort into them, but I also pick my battles (and
  passions). Nietzsche (1974) states, "Know
  thyself," which also means knowing what's
  worth doing and whether it will pay off.

- *Challenge making assumptions about yourself,
  people, and situations.* You never know what you
  are capable of until you're doing it. I think
  many people are surprised at how resourceful
  they are when the need truly arises. See in
  yourself and other people a potential for
  growth in a new situation rather than a fixed
  reaction. That way, you can come to each new
  situation informed but not close-minded.

- *Recognize that past negative life experiences don't
  determine the future that lies ahead of you.* This is
  a crucial one for me. Alfred North Whitehead
  attests that all of reality is basically flux;
  something is moving all the time, and nothing

is still. For Whitehead, time is the process of
things becoming themselves. You don't
become who you are (per Nietzsche) in one
day or even one year; we make mistakes along
the way, and we keep making mistakes.
However, we make less mistakes, and we fail
better at them.

My friend, Ben, has a little bit of a fixed mindset. I was
waiting bars with him when we both felt the impact of
the economic recession. Suddenly, small-plate restau-
rants in hip neighborhoods with cocktails no longer
seemed like the cash cow they used to be. I realized I
had to adapt to the new economic environment, so I
joined another friend, Greg, in his garage to work on
motorcycles. However, Ben insisted he had to keep
waiting tables at the same restaurant.

"Why?" I asked.

"It's all I know how to do," said Ben. "I've been here
since Day One."

"You know, Ben," I began. "You could sell anything. I
remember when you sold that couple a..."

"...forty-seven-dollar cocktail served out of a glass shoe
with a parasol!"

"Exactly," I laughed. "I thought that was just a novelty item. Maybe you should aim somewhat higher and sell something else."

Ben became a real estate agent and is now a millionaire. Let me offer an alternative example, however. Greg, my motorcycle mechanic friend, has a penchant for helping people. He works with his church to bring food to the needy. He is growth-oriented since he taught himself to be a mechanic and did not let any initial blown gaskets discourage him. He is open-minded too. One day, he realized that one of the beneficiaries of the church's money was using it for a purpose other than food. Apparently, this fund recipient had plenty of food, was not in need, and was, therefore, exploiting others. Greg had to make a tough decision; he decided his moral opposition to injustice meant that this recipient would no longer receive church funds, even though the Bible also states that we should give those claiming to be needy the benefit of the doubt. A reversion to a fixed mindset is sometimes warranted when moral issues arise that threaten your basic understanding of right and wrong. It's not that we can't repent for crimes or become new people, but in the midst of injustice, it's important to not lose our moral compass in the name of being open to new experiences.

How are you doing down that road? You have seen a lot in a short time: moral dilemmas, sublime sights, dreary deserts, and beautiful pastures. You have learned what it takes to challenge some of your negative thinking. Henry Ford once said, "Whether you think you can, or you think you can't—you're right" ("Henry Ford quotes," 2022). In the next chapter, I will talk about overcoming self-doubt on your way to becoming a more self-confident man.

6

CONQUERING FEAR AND SELF-DOUBT

I don't know any man who has not doubted himself. Perhaps you do, but I doubt it. Every man I know has gone through a period of his life where he thought he wasn't going to make it in his dreams, his aspirations, his values, and so forth. She is not a man, but even Mother Teresa had a crisis of faith. I think we can all relate to the feeling that we're not going to make it, despite all the efforts we put into our aspirations. Let's get rid of this feeling now.

I stated that everyone experiences feelings of self-doubt, men and women both. The reason is because we are realistic animals; I cannot do certain things despite whatever training or aspirations I have about them. I cannot go to the moon, for instance, because I'm not fit enough (for one reason). Doubt comes from the same place as anxiety; it is an evolutionary disposition to danger. Charles S. Peirce puts forth an interesting hypothesis; he says doubt is the disruption of the continuity of understanding of things. We only doubt when we question something that is in front of us, such as regular life that is suddenly disturbed. We only question something when we are given a reason to doubt. Doubt, therefore, is not a noun as much as a verb; it's something we do in life that comes with a life where we take risks.

Like anxiety, too much doubt keeps you from reaching your true potential. Doubt leads us to avoid situations where we might take risks because we're afraid of what could happen. Maybe you, dear reader, are afraid of success. That's not uncommon among the men I talk to.

Before I speak about how to overcome self-doubt (and gain self-confidence), I would like to state three points that are worth pondering on before I proceed:

- *Acknowledge your fear.* Realizations don't come often; we are not the prophets from ages past. At the same time, an understanding of what we are going through will take us a long way toward healing our traumas and becoming more confident. Remember what Confucius says: by calling something by its name, we understand it. This includes your fear(s).

- *Face your fear(s).* This is not easy. I have not faced every fear I have. Some of my fears are material; I don't like snakes, though I'm okay with spiders. Other fears are existential; I worry about failure. I have doubts. I think, "Maybe no one wants to read my book," but here you are reading it. The fact is many of our doubts are not correspondent to reality; rather, they are a product of neurosis, not the kind of understanding which Peirce describes that doubt is before we take action. Doubt turns into (self-)understanding when we take action to rectify the understanding and don't let a lack of it overwhelm our lives.

- *Self-doubt and imposter syndrome go hand in hand.* I mentioned imposter syndrome in Chapters 1, 2, and 4. This condition will come back into play in this chapter. I guarantee that many of the most successful people you know have thought they don't deserve the success they have. Not to toot my own horn, but I had three years working in a position of relative power. The amount of neurosis—not meant as a scientific term here—I observed was shocking.

The people who think they belong least are the ones that most belong.

Now that I have gotten these points out of the way, let us proceed to the meat of this chapter. You want to know how to overcome self-doubt. This is one way to gain self-confidence, after all. Think of doubt in the "clinical" sense I described earlier (from Peirce); it is a break in understanding that helps you understand more things about the world. I will teach you how to diminish doubt but also how to use it to your benefit.

- *Practice self-compassion.* I think we forget how human we are in the rat race that is life in the 21st century. As Nietzsche (1974) says, we are "human, all too human." An understanding of our limitations can help us foster a position of compassion toward ourselves and others. Perhaps we have compassion toward others, but not ourselves. Unfortunately, this is common among many of the men I meet. I think it's important to realize that we make mistakes, and mistakes are what help us grow. I already stated that no self-realization occurs without error. You are still reading because I'm sure that you have not been able to prove me wrong.

- *Remember your past achievements.* Do you remember times when you were scared something would go wrong, but it ended up going okay? Maybe it was even good? I have had many of these experiences. In fact, most of my experiences were this way because I suffered from anxiety and underestimated myself. I always anticipated the worst (which is not a poor evolutionary strategy, but an exhausting one) and usually got something okay or even pleasantly surprising. Perhaps you can relate to this outcome. An author at Eugene Therapy states that "something challenging turns us into something great" ("10 tips to overcome..," 2020, para. 8). They add, "Achievements are born out of initial uncertainty or doubt" ("10 tips to overcome...," 2020). I could not say it better myself. Neither could Peirce, actually. Remember that things have gone right before, so what stops them from going right again? The present moment is your opportunity to do well. This relates to the lesson of mindfulness.

- *Try not to compare yourself to others.* As the saying goes, comparison is the thief of joy. I remember, about 10 years ago, when I decided to stop comparing myself to others because I realized that it didn't matter. Of course, I still use other people as inspiration. Leonardo da Vinci accomplished a lot, so did Nikola Tesla, George Carver Washington, and Marie Curie. Do you think they compared themselves to the contemporaries of their time or simply let their doubt fuel their curiosity? I know a little bit about Tesla; if he stopped at the first failed experiment, we would not have alternating current.

- *Be mindful of your thinking.* You've heard about mindfulness before, not only in this book, but elsewhere. It is not a fad, but rather a foundation of thinking. I think we may not always recognize our negative thoughts because some of us have them so often. Imposter syndrome thrives off this negativity. We feel we aren't worthy of the place that we're in or are incapable of performing optimally. These are just thoughts. Next time these thoughts persist, ask them if they're true. Thoughts are not true automatically, just like statements are not true automatically. "I love my purple unicorn" is a statement, but it is not *true* because there are no unicorns that are purple in this world (or of any color). A shift to positive thinking may shift your mindset (see Chapter 5) into one that will allow you to be more self-confident with your abilities.

- *Spend time with supportive people.* If there is no greater treasure in life than friendship, then family is the bounty of treasure. Our family members and those that believe in us will generally always be on our side. It is on the onus of us to surround ourselves with people who bring light into our life. We should seek out people who are talented and resourceful, who are resilient and there for us in hard times. These people are rare, but they are valuable. If you find one (including in your family), hold on to them.

- *Find validation within.* I already mentioned that no amount of beautiful women on yachts telling me "I'm special" will make me feel like I'm special. I admit, it will make me feel special for a little while (the time I'm on the yacht and shortly after). But then, I have to go home, to a house or a studio apartment, it doesn't matter. It's not a yacht. I am alone with my thoughts and copy of Aurelius's *Meditations*. I have to love who I am to be myself at home and in a dream like the one I described. It's important that we have faith in ourselves. As in the case of the yacht-women, "Consistent reassurance doesn't

mean much if we don't believe in ourselves"
("10 tips to overcome...," 2020, para. 13).

- *Recall that you're your harshest critic.* I asked in
  Chapter 3 if you would doubt a friend like you
  doubt yourself. Self-love is about having a
  friendship with yourself. You give your friends
  the benefit of the doubt; this you should also
  give yourself. I had a friend who started a
  business, but it wasn't successful. In retrospect,
  I should have said something. I should have
  said, "Edward, you're not going to make it how
  you think you're going to make it. I appreciate
  the gusto, though." What did Edward do? He
  failed, but he learned a lesson; he's not a
  millionaire like Ben, but he's smarter with his
  investments. If Edward tells me, "Andrew, I
  think I have a business idea," do you know what
  I would answer? "Tell me. I want to hear
  about it."

- *Identify your values.* There are some things about
  you that are good. Some of us believe we are
  made in God's image. If we are not made that
  way, then we are still not all bad (at least I
  believe that). Some of us value kindness. Some
  of us value friendship. Some of us value ruthless
  competition. I will say it straight out; there is
  something to admire in all sorts of men. The

challenge is finding a balance that works in a society that is increasingly less accommodating to traditional forms of masculinity. In any case, men and women alike feel better when we live aligned with our values. It doesn't feel as bad to get criticized or to make a mistake when we believe in what we're doing; it's only a setback to an overall goal that motivates us. Better yet, it's a learning opportunity (see point 7).

- *Keep a journal.* I am a fan of music, if that's not evident in my writing. The reason is expressed by Arthur Schopenhauer, who believes music is a substrate of the Will, which means that it is the only art form that mimics life enough to take us away from its pains. There is a lyric from El-P, in a song titled, "Delorean," where he brags that his opponents' lyrics "hit like teddy bears thrown against wooden doors / by a misunderstood teenage girl in a moment of self-importance" (Meline, 2002). I found it ironic that El-P's diss of his fellow rappers is basically an exercise in journaling, as is any expressive art form. If you think keeping a diary is for teenage girls, consider other ways to express your emotions beyond talking with a therapist (see tip 10), such as through painting, music, dance, and poetry.

- *Seek professional help.* It may be hard to admit that we need help. It was for me, at least. I was raised to believe men should be self-sufficient and self-sustaining "islands." In a way, that is true—we do care for people who need help—but, similar to owning a motorcycle, we all need the human equivalent of an oil change or a tune-up eventually. You don't want to be riding on a hog that breaks down on a country road. A therapist may be the key to keeping your oil fresh. At the least, a therapist is a neutral arbiter who is paid to listen to your feelings and comment intelligently on them. If you buy your friend a beer at the bar, it may be therapeutic, but I can't promise you intelligence.

I have talked about imposter syndrome in previous chapters. In this chapter, I want to relate imposter syndrome to my own experiences, and perhaps yours. Rather, I will not just talk about my own experiences, but the experiences of my colleagues. Let us say I worked in a fairly high-powered firm. It wasn't a business firm, so the kind of people I was meeting weren't businessmen. Rather, it was in a scientific industry where I met many credentialed people; they were all from the schools you expect. To a tee, almost all of them suffered from imposter syndrome.

Let's review. Imposter syndrome is the belief that you are undeserving of your achievements and high self-esteem. You feel as though you aren't as competent or intelligent as others. Most tellingly (in terms of "diagnosing" imposter syndrome), you feel like people will uncover your "secrets." I talked a bit about these secrets in Chapter 3.

The fact is that imposter syndrome affects the more well-accomplished. It affects those who hold high offices or have numerous academic degrees. It certainly affected my colleagues.

I noticed in my discussions with these people that they would "continually attribute their accomplishments to external or transient causes." These causes included luck, good training, or "effort that cannot be regularly expended" ("Imposter syndrome," 2022, para. 2). At times, it seemed like I was the only person who felt like he deserved to be there, and I was suffering from low self-confidence.

The fact is that a competitive environment contributes to our feeling of imposter syndrome and low self-confidence. Is competition inherently bad? I don't think so, but that's just my opinion. I think competition fosters some of our best instincts. So does cooperation, of course, in certain cases. Like some of our best insights come from our mistakes, some of our best accomplishments come from being challenged by ourselves and others.

According to a study, 25-30% of high achievers report suffering from imposter syndrome ("Imposter syndrome," 2022). Some of our symptoms of imposter syndrome may be related to what we were taught in childhood. In short, if we were taught to have a fixed mindset (see Chapter 5), we may be more prone to imposter syndrome.

Maybe you can relate to my experiences of imposter syndrome at my firm. Even amongst others that suffered the same thing, I never took the time to reward myself for doing anything right. I always focused on the negatives. I always looked ahead and to the next challenge, instead of taking a break and rewarding myself.

I already stated that mistakes are part of our growing experience. Perhaps if you are experiencing imposter syndrome, you should seek out a mentor who has gone through the same thing. You may be surprised how many of your colleagues and friends have also felt like an imposter. Ellen Hendricksen outlines some signs of imposter syndrome:

- *You think, "I'm a fraud."* Hendricksen (2017, para. 5-6) provides examples of employees who state that "everyone else at that table has earned their place except me," or "this place isn't for people like me. I don't belong here." I wonder how many people at the table, in the case of the first example, are thinking the same thing.

- *You attribute your success solely to luck.* Hendricksen (2017, para. 8) quotes an employee who states, "I was in the right place at the right time." Everyone who has succeeded relied on a little bit of luck and (typically) a lot of effort.

- *You can't take a compliment.* Hendricksen (2017, para. 11) quotes a student as stating, "I got a good grade because it was easy," and "That swim meet I won wasn't really important." An employee even said, "No one else applied— that's why I got the job" (Hendricksen, 2017).

What are the causes of imposter syndrome? I have listed them below:

- *You're told that you're amazing all the time.* According to Hendricksen (2017, para. 13), "Well-meaning parents over-praise their kids by showering them with compliments." The compliment of intelligence is "flattering but implies that there is nowhere left to go," according to this author (Hendricksen, 2017). Furthermore, "smart" is zero-sum; you either are, or you're not. Being called smart decreases your willingness to try new things, as the results might contradict the label of "smart." Instead, parents should praise effort and creativity to foster a growth mindset in their children.

- *You're a racial minority or other marginalized person.* Being an "Other" in the society of a monolithic culture may make you feel like you're illegitimate or fake. You may lack a mentor or role model who looks like you or has had your experiences. For example, first-generation achievers may feel like they don't fit into the society or with their parents. As society changes, what determines being marginal also changes. We can feel marginal in situations where we would otherwise be dominant.
- *It's a side effect of meritocracy.* As Hendricksen (2017, para. 18) states, "High achievers are only high achievers compared to others." Meritocracy values the process of comparison because it has done well by it in the past. However, there is a limit in this approach of valuing people. From the individual's perspective, too much awareness of yourself in a meritocratic system can be detrimental. You may think too much and cause yourself anxiety.

In this chapter, I want to talk about how to combat imposter syndrome before I move to perfectionism and eliminating self-doubt. Take these steps if you are experiencing imposter syndrome:

- *Recognize that your feelings are normal.* From honor students to Nobel Prize winners, everyone experiences imposter syndrome. I started Chapter 3 by talking about my "secret." Everyone has something to hide, and when you have imposter syndrome, you think you are the only one with a secret.
- *Recall your previous accomplishments.* If you have a resume, write a *curriculum vitae* (which lists accomplishments besides your job). Read old letters of recommendation to yourself. Remember that you do not just look good on paper; you are a real person who accomplished all that which is written down.
- *Tell someone about what you're going through.* Disclose your feelings to a trusted friend, teacher, or colleague. You may be surprised what kind of insight you get. Be careful to not overwhelm someone and keep the conversation on track about imposter syndrome.
- *Seek out a mentor.* I mentioned this already, but is there a guide who matches your spirit?

Someone you look up to or admire? Seek them out.

- *Teach!* Become a mentor yourself. You'll be surprised how much you can share with others. When we become an expert on something, we are conscious about how much more we have to learn. Getting good at something may amplify our feelings of fraudulence; teaching others about what we are passionate about can put our abilities into perspective.
- *Know that it's okay to not know what you're doing.* We don't all know what we're doing the first time. In fact, none of us do. As Hendricken (2017, para. 28) states, "As long as you are enthusiastic about learning, people will cut you slack."
- *Praise your children's effort.* To promote a growth mindset in your children, make sure to praise effort and creativity rather than innate talents. You should say, "You worked so hard on that" and "You didn't give up, even when it wasn't working out," instead of "You're so smart!"
- *Expect initial failure.* As Hendricksen (2017, para. 27) states, "Here's your new bike. You have to fall off 10 times before you get good."
- *Keep a little imposter syndrome in your pocket.* Authentic modesty, when you get good at

something and know your limitations, will keep you grounded. Remember your past; recall what your experiences with imposter syndrome were like before you started to gain your self-confidence.

Shonna Waters discusses the phenomenon of perfectionism, which is related to imposter syndrome and is typically experienced by high achievers. Perfectionism is a symptom of low self-confidence. As Waters (2022, para. 1) states, "Perfection doesn't exist—it doesn't stop us from trying to reach it." A disposition toward perfectionism may initially make you work harder and smarter, but there is a limit to these effects. In general, workers who crave perfection tend to work more but produce less. A self-confident man realizes he is worthy, valuable, and capable regardless of his success. He knows this because he has succeeded in the past and will succeed in the future.

Causes of perfectionism include the following:

- feelings of inadequacy and fear of disapproval
- underlying OCD and/or anxiety disorder
- a parent or guardian that encourages it
- attachment issues from absent parental figures

Like there are ways to overcome imposter syndrome, there are also ways to overcome perfectionism. Waters lists several:

- *Focus on the positives.* Perfectionism makes us focus on the negatives in our lives. This makes sense as an evolutionary strategy, but it is not good for our mental health in the contemporary era. Emphasizing your positives and strengths is the first step to overcoming perfectionism.
- *Allow yourself to make mistakes.* Mistakes teach us about life and ourselves, and they help us grow. As Waters (2022, para. 40) puts it, "Our most remarkable accomplishments result from our worst mistakes."
- *Set reasonable goals.* Unrealistic expectations set us up for failure before we even begin. Goals should be realistic and attainable. When making goals, be realistic about what you can achieve and how much effort you can put in. Practice self-compassion for yourself. After all, things don't always go according to plan. Finally, don't beat yourself up if you put your best efforts forward.
- *Find meaning in what you're doing.* If we're passionate about the work we do, we care less

about doing it "perfectly" and more about doing it right. Right is not the same thing as perfect. A job you are passionate about is less prone to perfectionism and is also more fun.

- *Cut out negative influences from your life.* Believing resting or having shortcomings is "toxic" is a consequence of "hustle culture," according to Waters (2022, para. 44). In fact, we all need rest and have shortcomings. Waters recommends limiting the amount of time spent consuming media or being around people who negatively impact your mental health.

- *Go to therapy*! Therapy will help you lift your burdens off your shoulders. You can talk to someone and not worry about judgment. That is a precious service.

One reason we do not always accomplish what we set out to do is because of limiting beliefs. According to Tony Robbins (2022, para. 4), limiting beliefs are the "stories we tell about ourselves." These beliefs limit us from reaching our full potential.

Robbins (2022, para 5) claims that the human brain is "wired" to conserve energy. We seek certainty in our routines, relationships, and jobs. We are averse to risk and don't always go outside of our comfort zones.

According to Robbins (2022, para. 5), "We invest energy into taking actions we believe will produce results." If we think we will not produce the results, we stop before we even try. Sabotaging our brain is the consequence of these limiting beliefs. Robbins lists common limiting beliefs:

- *I don't have time.* As the saying goes, when you truly care about something, you find time for it. Robbins (2022, para. 7) says, "Everyone has the same hours in a day. It's what you do with it that matters." I guarantee you you can find time for what you really wanted if the desire presents itself to you that day.
- *I don't have what it takes.* We all have a fear of failure. Some of us have a fear of success, due to deep psychological reasons related to a fear of failure. Perhaps we tell ourselves, "I could do that, but I don't have the skills." We can engender the skills to do many things with enough effort.
- *I'm not strong enough.* This thought keeps us in our comfort zone. We need inner strength to comfort us during rejection, failure, or discomfort. If you're not feeling this way now, these feelings are inevitable in the future. As Robbins (2022, para. 9) puts it, "We would

rather stay where we are than risk getting
hurt."

- *I don't deserve love.* If we believe this, we may
  reject every potential partnership.

Living in fear leads to perfectionism, settling, procrastination, and numbing yourself, according to Robbins.
Perfectionism is a mask we wear to protect ourselves
from finding an intimate connection. Likewise, settling
comes from a need for certainty in life. Procrastination
allows us to keep making excuses. Numbing yourself is
self-explanatory; you don't need drugs or alcohol to get
through life.

Robbins outlines five steps to stop living in fear and
lower your self-doubt.

- Identify what you're actually afraid of.
- Find situations that are mildly uncomfortable
  but not panic-inducing.
- Be realistic—what are the worst consequences
  of your action?
- Visualize yourself being successful.
- Take action and put yourself out there!

In this chapter, I gave you the tools to lower your self-
doubt and raise your self-confidence, but you cannot
cultivate these tools until you put them to use. In the

next chapter, I discuss being your own champion, so you can go out into the world with confidence, instead of meekness. I think we're almost out of the forest now. Do you see the end of the trees? Frost's road was winding and ragged; obviously, there were easier ways to go. We didn't go those ways though. You don't want to stop before you see what's on the other side, do you?

7

BECOMING YOUR OWN CHAMPION

W hat's on the other side of the forest? There is an improved man with greater self-confidence and an easier life. After all, life *becomes* easier with the right attitude, as Marcus Aurelius claims. I talked about changing your mindset in Chapter 5. Here, put your positive mindset to good use and hold yourself as your number one priority in a productive and social way by becoming your own champion.

Part of becoming your own champion is protecting your time and energy from "vampires." This anti-vampire defense mechanism includes saying "no" to people when they ask you to do things that don't suit you. A self-confident man expresses his needs and feelings in an authentic way, and so does someone who champions himself.

As I argued in the last chapter, to achieve self-confidence, you must make conscious choices to face your fears and doubts. Sometimes, it's difficult to stand up for ourselves, but it's never impossible. Once we learn to be our own champion, we can truly have control of our lives.

A writer at Achieve Medical Center notes that "minutes to yourself are few and far between" ("How to protect...," 2022, para. 1). I think many people can relate to the feeling that we don't have words to spare at the end of the day. Perhaps we are pulled in a thousand directions; as this author ("How to protect...," 2022) states, "Everyone is in crisis; they come to you."

According to this author ("How to protect...," 2022, para. 2), it is "our nature to help ease pain and worries of those close to us." Beneath this positivity, however, may be exhaustion. As this writer ("How to protect...," 2022) states, "You don't have to be everyone's superman." This writer at Achieve Medical Center offers some ways to avoid time-vampires (the other type of vampire saps energy):

- *Set clear and firm boundaries.* According to this author ("How to protect…," 2022, para. 5), "Self-preservation is a challenging task." You have to be there for your friends and family. Beyond "having" to be there for them, we often *want* to. At the same time, these people have to be independent as well, whether they are family or friends; they have to be able to take care of themselves. *Agape*—which is a classification of love written about by Ancient Greeks and in the Bible—is a kind of love that desires what's best for another person, even if they don't want it. The point of establishing boundaries is to foster *agape* between you and the rest of humanity—it's not to let them down.

- *Set aside time for you.* You don't have to answer your phone all the time. In fact, you can turn *off* your phone. More realistically, you can turn off your phone for a designated period of time (and set it on your work calendar). As this author states, "See how it feels to be alone; you may like it" ("How to protect…," 2022, para. 7). As they also point out, there is a difference between alone time and isolation. Alone time is precisely to recharge after we engage in social interaction; social interaction is necessary for us whether we are introverts or extroverts.

- *Recognize your emotions.* Those who are compelled to help others are often experts at compartmentalizing or suppressing emotions. As this author ("How to protect...," 2022, para. 8), states, "Train yourself to respond and not react." Men, especially, often "turn off" our feelings. This suppression may manifest as physical aches and pains, as it did for me. Your body stores feelings you forget about, often in your hips. We need to strike a balance between being too open and too firm; a calm collectedness combines the best elements of both dispositions.

- *Limit your exposure to negativity.* I think it's often good advice to "listen to what your body is telling you" ("How to protect...," 2022). You do not have to engage in a situation if you don't want to. If you don't want to engage in a situation, and have no reason to, then you probably shouldn't. It's perfectly okay—and in fact preferable—to excuse yourself and leave the room if you don't like what's going on. There are some things in this world we can control. You can't control the situation, but you can control how you react.

I talked about one type of vampire already: a time-vampire. There is at least one other type of vampire who is competing for your soul: an energy-vampire. Think about what a vampire is. In Brad Stoker's *Dracula*, one of the myths that Stoker puts forward is that a vampire has to be let into your house for the evil to be effective. Likewise, time- and energy-vampires "ask" to be let into your life and stay there (whether it is explicitly or through work or social obligations). Unlike the vampires of Stoker's mythology, these soul-sucking vampires can be removed.

Jordan Gray offers tips for how to protect your time. Gray (2016, para. 2) states, "Your life is full of time-vampires." Among these tips are

- *Figure out your core values.* I talked already about having a *Weltanschauung*; these are the values that are nonnegotiable, even in a growth mindset. Sticking to your core values ensures you don't lose time which will make you resentful.
- *Put big things on your calendar.* As Gray (2016, para. 12) states, "If you fill up a bowl with sand, there's no room for tennis balls." If you fill up a bowl with tennis balls first, there is still room for sand. The tennis balls are important; the sand is everything else.

- *Figure out your overarching "Nos"*. If you know what you're not willing to do, you won't burn out on decision fatigue. Examples of overarching "Nos" include no alcohol or meeting up for drinks, no calls or meetings before noon, no to anything that interrupts date night, and so forth. When someone asks you to do something you are uncomfortable with (see first bullet), say, "I don't do X, Y, or Z," rather than, "Mm… not this time." The latter opens you up to be disrespected by the same request sometime in the future.

- *Say "no" politely*. Politeness is defined by Gray as good manners mixed with clarity. Consider that saying "no" is not about the other person— usually. Perhaps you are simply busy. Make the requester understand your declination isn't about them. When saying "no," add, "I hope you understand." This puts the onus of decision-making on the requester, and there is a new decision to be made: either they understand or not that you would not do it.

- *Think of the ultimate cost of decisions*. Gray writes (2016, para. 26), "Every minute has infinite uses." Any minute you use for something can be used for something else. This is called an opportunity cost in economics. Ask yourself:

what do you gain from a given experience?
What else could you do with your time? This is
called A-B testing. You can only do one thing,
so which thing is best to do?

- *Prioritize core values above all else, consistently.*
Gray implores you to pick what matters and
optimize for that. Like the tennis balls and sand
in the bowl example, other things you want to
do can be put into your schedule after meeting
your primary goals and aspirations.

- *Have sacred time in the day.* "Guard your
mornings against time-vampires," writes Gray
(2016, para. 41). I agree with him. The
mornings are only for me. I do yoga. I listen to a
podcast. I don't check my emails. I don't take
work calls. If you want to steal my time,
schedule it after I've had my coffee.

Gray contends that saying "no" is what differentiates
his clients who make between six and seven figures and
those who make nine. In the case of the nine-figure
earners, "Nothing gets in the way of their priorities,"
states Gray (2016, para. 45). Saying "no" is about
expressing our feelings. We can express our feelings
and needs directly and respectfully. Moreover, talking
about our feelings helps with emotional regulation. In
other words, talking about ourselves does not feel like a

regulatory process as it occurs, but it is, and it makes us feel better. That's why, whether with a friend or a therapist, we like talking about ourselves.

Kit Stone emphasizes the importance of clarity in communication. She points out that "what you communicate to doctors is essential to how doctors care for you" (Stone, 2019, para. 3). She notes that "high expectations without communication will just bring hardship into a relationship" (Stone, 2019, para. 6). What stops people from speaking is the fear of how we will be perceived and how our speech affects other people. According to Stone (2019, para. 16), "The ability to ask what we want is an essential life skill." Asking is important because it "eliminates assumptions and promotes authentic communication." (Stone, 2019)

Here are four ways to communicate openly and honestly (particularly as a self-confident man):

- *Describe your observations.* Say what you notice around you from your point of view. Make factual statements about the world around you. For example, you could say, "I see you were late for our date by thirty minutes. You said you would be here at 8 p.m. but arrived at 8:30. I felt bad about that because I thought you were taking my time for granted. Can you be more mindful of my time during our next date?"

- *Name how your situation makes you feel.* I alluded to this above. Make "I" statements. "'I' feel bad that you arrived late. 'I' always make an effort to arrive on time because 'I' value your time," and so forth.

- *State what you need.* State that it's important for your date to arrive on time and (perhaps) put her phone away for the date. You want quality time with this person. This requirement starts with arriving when you say you will; at least, where I come from, this promptness is important. There are gentler ways to express this to a date, but you get the idea.

- *Make specific requests.* "Can you please text me if you're going to be late?" is an action item you can pursue. Likewise, "Can you be on time next time?" will work. If you don't specify what's wrong, the other person won't be able to guess. Maybe they'll guess, and they'll guess wrong.

An honest conversation can benefit you and the other person, even if it feels uncomfortable at first. Honesty helps us understand each other at a deeper level. Open communication is a bit like saying, "Let me help you." Everyone wants to hear that.

Stone (2019, para. 29) recommends that if you "give someone what they need; they are more likely to give you what you need in return." I'm not so sure about that. I was never sold on karma, though its principles hold sometimes. A self-confident man cannot count on his good deeds being reciprocated. That is why a self-confident man does things for their intrinsic, rather than their instrumental, value. I talked earlier about how what is external becomes internal for the self-confident man. Likewise, what we do has value In-itself rather than just value-for-Others (to momentarily adopt Sartrean language). The fact is, a man with confidence is driven toward the good, and his intrinsic activities help others. I disagree that men are primarily driven by altruism; our altruism is a consequence of our integrity and creativity.

Jeanna Britton (2019, para. 1) attests that "friendships can be as deep (even deeper) than relationships," echoing Plato who exalted love and friendship in his *Symposium*. Critically, Plato—through his avatar of Socrates—contends that friendship is only possible between equals. Consider this as I go through ways to improve communication in friendships (and romantic relationships).

It's hard to ask for help without feeling needy. Perhaps it's hard to ask for help at all, and that's why we wait until the last moment to do so. It's possible to communicate our needs in a position of strength and mutual reliance with our friends. Think about what Plato says: friendship is about *equality*. Below are some pointers to follow when having clear communication:

- *Be clear about what's on your mind.* People can't read your mind. As I stated earlier, if they try to guess, they might guess it wrong. Know that "what we want" and "what we need" are two different things (as the Rolling Stones [1969] song goes, "You can't always get what you want."). Consider your potential date above; she arrived 30 minutes late. How does her flakiness make you feel? Perhaps it's not a big deal. Thirty minutes may turn into an hour if nothing is said. Whoever is meeting you for a coffee or drink needs to know that you must be a priority in their life; otherwise, you wouldn't have agreed to the date.

- *Be intentional in your communication or schedule a time to discuss intentionally.* Sometimes it's actually not a good time to tell someone what's on your mind. Perhaps they're busy, or they have something on their mind. Schedule a time where you can both be ready to discuss. No excuses.

- *Don't be accusatory.* By being honest and open, you're not accusing someone of something they did wrong (even if they did do something wrong)—rather, you're stating how you feel. If your interlocutor gets defensive (which often means they did something wrong), then remind them you're only stating how you feel. This is the difference between "You never make time for me!" vs. "I feel like I'm not a priority in your life."

- *Offer to return the favor.* You could state that, "I can help you with X if you can help me with Y." X is important to them; Y is important to you. This approach shows that you are thinking about the other person and can remember important things about them. This may catch them off guard and allow them to open up a little more.

As Britton (2019, para. 10) puts it, "Being clear around people about what we want is a form of kindness." A "relationship is a careful dance of managing needs," Britton (2019, para. 13) continues, between "what it means to take up space and feel worthy" and our care for other people. This dance, for men, is a delicate one indeed.

Laken Howard (2017, para. 2) states that "many people aren't even consciously aware of what their emotional or sexual needs are." Howard (2017, para. 4) adds, "It takes courage to have an honest conversation."

I will state this axiomatically: you're worthy of having your needs met. It's important to talk to your partner about your needs. If your partner cares for you, they should be delighted and open to learn more about you. Describe an ideal relationship to yourself and your partner—what does it look like? What actionable steps can you take to realize some perfection on Earth— knowing that we are all limited by our earthliness?

In a romantic relationship or friendship, don't be too intimidated to voice your concerns. The last thing you want to do is bottle up your feelings. You will grow resentful and the feelings will come out somehow, sooner or later. It's better to be honest from the beginning to avoid that down the line.

Think about your feelings in a somewhat neutral or "clinical" way. Ask yourself the following:

- What is this feeling?
- What does this feeling tell me about the situation?
- Why is this feeling happening now?

- What is my body doing in response to this feeling?

Once you realize what you're feeling, you can take steps to address a potential lack or gap between reality and your expectations. What can you do to feel better? Will you do it?

We need to remember that emotions are not analogous to the truth. Often, when men deal with intense emotions, we are either expressing them toward someone (often in anger) or suppressing them until it hurts us. In terms of the outbursts or the suppression, we can ask the following:

- What result am I hoping for with my outburst or suppression?
- What do I want to do about my feelings?
- What if I do nothing?

You are an adult. You have options (now). You can eat McDonalds every day and finish it up with ice cream if you really want to (even though you shouldn't). If something in your life isn't working, you have the ability to change it. No one is in charge of your life but you. Think about the last question, "What if I do nothing?" This is a powerful option we often do not consider. Sometimes, the best approach is not to do the same thing that has gotten us into trouble in the past, but actually stop doing it entirely. Is that simple enough?

Kasey van Dyke attests that we avoid emotions, in part, because they are tied in with tough topics. "Some experiences are too big or traumatic for us to talk about," van Dyke (2021, para. 7) adds. Moreover, "Trauma makes it harder to describe our feelings," so we are at a disadvantage when speaking about tough topics at all (van Dyke, 2021, para. 9). Social norms and sexual abuse can contribute to our lack of openness. Sometimes, it seems like the whole world is opposed to our existence.

Studies show that it is "far easier than you think to be sociable in positive, low-pressure situations" (van Dyke, 2021, para. 19). Think about your own experiences. Even if you're shy and suffer from low self-confidence, there are situations where you would feel perfectly at ease. Think about your hobbies; maybe you are a Pokémon collector. Even if you have difficulty speaking to others, I bet you could muster some excitement about Pokémon.

Beyond simply discussing our feelings, there are ways to optimize talking about our feelings when we do choose to talk about them. You can try

- taking deep breaths
- practicing to talk with friends and family
- identifying and accepting your emotions before you start talking
- finding the right listener for the right moment or conversation

You can't talk to just anyone. Talk to someone who understands what you're going through (as much as possible). Your aunt may understand your life trajectory but not your depressive symptoms. Your closest friend may understand your depressive symptoms even if she's never seen you in diapers. There is also another approach; you can help someone else express their feelings, like your best friend. Express to them that you are there to help too. A good listener turns into a better talker naturally.

Let us review how to say "no." You have your core values, your *Weltanschauung*. You are open and flexible but don't want to cross your fundamental boundaries. You are confident (at least a little more) that you are worthy and valuable in your own right. Why do we have trouble saying "no"? Erin Eatough (2022, para. 3) writes that "saying 'no' is packed with guilt." We are afraid of disappointing ourselves or others. Perhaps we are anxious to turn down our boss. Perhaps we are people-pleasers (see Chapter 4).

Growing up, we are taught that saying "no" is back talk. Maybe we are punished for it. However, we are also taught to be polite and forthcoming; this involves saying "no" to other people when it is appropriate. Human beings are social creatures. We require human connections and a need to belong. Saying "no" may threaten our sense of belonging within our greater community.

When do you say "no"? You should say "no" when

- You feel uncomfortable.
- You are doing something out of guilt or obligation (remember, your time is not less valuable than theirs).
- You're overloaded.
- The request crosses personal boundaries.
- You're doing it just to please someone else.

As I argued in Chapter 4, being a people-pleaser leads you to "do more and deliver less" (Eatough, 2022, para. 26). Eatough (2022, para. 27) writes that "being assertive pays off." This statement is true for me, but I will get to that story in another chapter. For now, try saying "no" to things you can't handle. In fact, don't *try* as much "do" (as Yoda declares in *Star Wars* [Lucas, 1977]). What's the worst that can happen? The alternative of not doing something is doing something badly.

I'm going to make a controversial statement: if you're going to do something badly, don't bother doing it at all (there are other people who can do it well, so leave it to them). Plato contends that we cannot believe in beautiful things without believing in the beautiful itself. You know that you are capable; you are capable of the things you are capable of. Do them well, and ask for help when needed. Cultivate your skills; don't focus on your limitations.

If someone invites you to an event that you don't want to go to, you can say, "That sounds fun, but..." or "I'm glad you want me there, though..." The last thing you want to do is stand around with your drink, alone, wishing you had the gumption to just say "no."

In the next chapter, I will talk about a topic near and dear to my heart: failure and how to move on from it with compassion.

8

TREAT YOURSELF WITH COMPASSION AND MOVE ON FROM FAILURE

I failed in life pretty spectacularly. I was given resources to get ahead, and I made good use of them for a while. I went to college, got a degree, made some investments, and got a good job. About three years into work, I picked up some bad habits that drained my finances. Next thing I knew, I was no longer saving but working from paycheck-to-paycheck. Then, I lost my job.

By the time I lost my job, I no longer had a family support structure. I was on my own. I worked odd jobs for a while: gas station attendant, gardener, motorcycle mechanic. Then, Ben brought me into his real estate business. I was crunching numbers and doing data analytics. Again, I'm not a math person—but statistics is a little easier. Four years after my downfall, I was making less at my new job than what I made at my first position. Was I any happier? Happiness depends on your interpersonal relations. I was certainly more confident, believe it or not.

Failure is a part of life, so why do we try so hard to avoid it? Failure doesn't feel good, first of all. I know this. In a sense, I admire people who have failed and turned their lives around. Some people admire me for the same reason. However, it's hard to admire failure as such, and that's a problem for society. There are two types of failures: honorable failures and incompetent failures. The latter is sad—though unavoidable—but the former is, in a way, impressive.

Susan Tardanico (2022, para. 3) writes correctly that "we hate to fail." She offers some tips for dealing with and moving on from failure:

- *Don't make it personal.* Separate failure from your identity. Just because you failed this one time does not mean you're a failure. In formal logic, this misattribution is called a transference fallacy. Maybe you haven't found a successful way of doing this one thing yet. Abraham Lincoln failed over a dozen times at trying to hold public office before he was elected Senator and then President.

- *Take stock, learn, and adapt.* Look at failure analytically and with curiosity. Ask yourself the following:

1. Why did you fail?
2. What might have produced better outcomes?
3. Was the failure beyond your control?

Thomas Edison failed 10,000 times before he invented the lightbulb. Each failure was a learning opportunity for him.

- *Stop dwelling.* Obsessing over failure will not change the outcome. Instead, it will only intensify the outcome by creating an "emotional doom-loop" (Tardanico, 2022, para. 10). We cannot change the past, but at least, we can change the future. It may be helpful to set a time limit for either brooding or celebrating; 24 hours may be enough to get your feelings out before you're ready to move on.
- *Release your need for the approval of others.* We often fear being judged and losing others' respect or esteem. Sometimes, this is for no good reason. We often get influenced and "spooked" about what people say about us (Tardanico, 2022, para. 12). You are in control

of your life, not them. What a person considers the truth may not be the truth at all. If you would like an artistic representation of this fact, watch Akira Kurasawa's film *Rashomon*.

- *Find a new point of view.* Consider that if you fail, you are one step closer to succeeding. When I fail, I become smarter and more savvy for next time. As Michael Jordan states, "I have failed over and over again in my life. And that is why I succeed" (Tardanico, 2022).

Paul Sloane (2022, para. 1) describes that "the best way to test an idea is not to analyze it but to try it." Many failures will often contribute to a mighty success. As Tom Kelley states, "Fail often to succeed sooner" (Sloane, 2022). Likewise, Soichiro Honda claims that "success represents the 1 percent of your work that results from the 99 percent that is called failure" (Sloane, 2022, para. 3). Honda should know this lesson well; he built an international car and motorcycle manufacturer starting from a wooden shack.

In discussing innovation in Silicon Valley, Sloane (2022, para. 4) claims that "failure is Silicon Valley's greatest strength." Sloane (2022) adds, "Every failure is a lesson stated in collective memory." You can learn from my mistakes like I can learn from yours. If we were all successful (which is impossible), we would have nothing to share and nothing to learn from each other.

I think it's important as a society that we stop stigmatizing failure; we must admire it for the effort. However, this is not a book about society; this is a book about *you*. You can get a head start and embrace your failures like you embrace your successes.

Sloane provides some tips for dealing with failure:

- *When you give people the freedom to succeed, you give them the freedom to fail.* Theologians from all religions often wonder why God gave us free will. In the Christian tradition, everything was fine in the Garden of Eden until Eve ate the forbidden fruit. After this, mankind was burdened with shame, sickness, and labor. Prior to the Fall, the only creatures with free will in God's kingdom were the angels, including Lucifer (who had previously composed music for God). One can see free will as a prison; we are no longer coddled by a benevolent Force, and we make choices that are often wrong. On the other hand, Lucifer and the other angels savored their free will. It is God's granting of free will to humans that ultimately made Lucifer rebel and set off into the underworld. It takes a tremendous amount of love—*agape*, in particular—to allow people to make their own mistakes. If God allowed this for you and me, then it makes sense to allow this for others and for yourself.

- *Differentiate honorable failure from incompetent failure.* Maybe you gave it your best shot. That is different from fudging it up. I talked in Chapter 5 about how we should raise children to be rewarded for their effort rather than the outcome. Congratulate yourself on the effort and see how the outcome can be improved for next time.

- *Boast about your failures. It's a learning experience.* I met a man, Trevor, who was a trader. Trevor bragged to me about losing three million dollars. My mouth dropped when he said this. "Aren't you *miserable*?" I asked. Trevor replied, "You have to make three million dollars, first, in order to lose it."

- *Consider each failure to be a methodology test.* In the sciences, before researchers (or universities, governments, and so forth) drop millions of dollars into research, they often fund a "pilot project" or a "proof of concept." This is a small version that is tested to see if the big thing is viable. If the pilot project does not work, we know how the major project may be adjusted. Or, we may learn it is not worth doing the major project at all; this is a research finding in its own right.

- *Experiment with what works.* Innovative leaders will encourage experimentation in their organizations. They know that out of "mad" ideas will come something brilliant, even if you have to sift through a lot of mud to get to the pearls. If you fail today, you could succeed tomorrow. Events are not always contingent on each other, even if they feel like they are. The only constant between yesterday and today is *you*.

Henrik Edberg offers a few more tips on dealing with failure:

- *Accept how you feel.* Do not be led away by your impulses when you are dealing with failure. Remember that suppressed emotions will "pop out at unexpected times" if they are not expressed at the appropriate time (Edberg, 2020, para. 13). You want to find a sweet spot between spiraling and ignoring how you feel; you need to accept how you feel and not let it take over.

- *Remember that you're not a failure.* Failure is a temporary state, not an ontological category. There is no such thing as failure in nature. If something is alive, that means it "works." Not only that, if something is alive, it means that its descendants have worked for millennia. Failure is only contingent on other options being evaluated. The mass extinction of human beings on Earth will be a "failure" for our race, but not the races of plants and animals that will take our place.

- *Be constructive and learn from a situation.* You're already in the situation. You may as well learn from it. Ask yourself the following questions:

1. What can I learn?
2. How can I adjust my course of action to avoid making the same mistakes?
3. What can I do differently next time?

- *Anyone who wants to do things of value in their life will fail.* It's easy enough to not be a "failure;" don't ever do anything important. Don't take up space. Apologize for your own existence. Never try anything hard. In essence, this life is *not* a failure (although it contains a lot of missed opportunities) because you never really tried. I would prefer to be like Michael Jordan, who led the Bulls to victory (and some defeats), rather than a player on the bench who never played a game. Who has more missed shots, Jordan or the bench-sitter? Jordan, of course. (Note that we mostly just hear about peoples' successes; Jordan has actively shared his failures!)

- *Let your failure out into the light.* Talk out your "failure" with someone close to you. This conversation will ground you in reality. When you are illuminated, you will illuminate the others around you. As I mentioned earlier, I think there's nothing lost in being open and honest; it helps you and your interlocutor.
- *Find inspiration and support from others.* Learn from those who went where you want to go. Read about how they handled their self-doubts and low points. I like to read, so I can read an inspiring book. You can listen to a podcast or watch a TV show or movie. Pick someone who inspires you and see what insight they provide.
- *Move forward; don't get stuck.* You failed (whatever that means). It's time to process and accept the event. It's easy to get stuck in thoughts, but it's even easier to move on with our day until we are able to deal with this trauma. For instance, I exercise or read a book

even when I'm stressed. I deal with the problem after, when I feel better.

- *Make a plan and stick with it.* Don't make your plan perfect. Divide your plan into small steps. Think about what will happen one week, one day, one hour, and five minutes in the future; plan for that. If you're going to fail (and you will), fail intelligently.

Now that you have some idea on how to approach failure, let's talk about specific coping skills you can use when confronted with a situation that doesn't go quite according to plan. Elizabeth Scott describes that procrastination, passive-aggressiveness, and rumination are all unhelpful coping strategies for dealing with failure. Avoidance coping, which is a change in behavior to avoid thinking about, feeling, or doing difficult things, also does not work—at least not in the long run. "Confronting problems is the only way to reduce stress," says Scott (2021, para. 4).

In other words, stress management is always going to be more optimal than stress avoidance. If you are avoiding a bear in the woods (I'm surprised we haven't met any bears on our journey!), then maybe "management" is the wrong word here. But let me put it this way: if you're going to go into the forest, you're going to see some bears. Some people have jobs in the forest, like loggers. Some people work around bears (God bless them!). These people all have to manage their bear-related stress, not just avoid it.

Consider procrastination. Procrastination does not make our stress about a deadline go away. Waiting longer to complete the work just magnifies the stress we have. Procrastination is a stress-generating activity, not a stress-relieving one.

There are healthy coping skills for dealing with experiences of failure, not just unhealthy ones. Healthy coping skills come in two forms: *problem-based coping* and *emotion-based coping*. The first form seeks to change your situation, remove stressful things from life, end relationships that are causing stress, and so forth. These are practical solutions to improve your circumstances right away. Emotion-based coping includes addressing the feelings you have when you're in the midst of failure or other stressful situations. This coping is useful when you can't change the situation you're in.

Consider getting a bad performance review at work. You're surprised you got a negative performance review because you thought you were doing a great job. Problem-based coping for this review includes talking to your boss. Why did you perform so poorly? You will only know if you ask. Then, you can develop a plan to improve your work. Emotion-based coping in this situation includes reading a book over lunch to destress, exercising, cleaning your home, or taking a long bath. Emotion-based coping is about making yourself calm until you're able to start implementing a plan through problem-based coping.

We all have to accept a level of responsibility for our actions. That is the curse of humanity; on the one hand, we are, in a minute way, not really responsible for our actions (after all, it was Lucifer himself who seduced Eve in the Garden of Eden), but we still have to claim responsibility for these actions. This outcome is, in a way, good; you don't want a society where everyone is excused from the consequences of what they do. Overcoming failure and being a more self-confident man is about fully accepting our role in our own successes and failures. Just like I had a major role in my failure, I had a major role in pulling myself out.

Kara Cufruzzula offers a few more tips for dealing with failure. She recommends the following:

- *Use a to-do list to build self-confidence.* We have to "get ourselves into the process of being brave," according to Cufruzzula (2020, para. 7). Fear is a signal that you care about the situation you're in. We can always do things around the margins in any situation, even if we cannot change it fundamentally.

- *Separate value from work.* Remember that you are not your work. In the midst of failure, ask: what can I learn? Work is not a reflection of your value; it is just one part of it.
- *Develop and depend on a mutual support group.* Cufruzzula writes that when we invest in someone, they will help us do more in the long term. Cufruzzula (2020) adds:

The more you shine, the more you light up everyone around you. While it can sometimes feel strange to share your accomplishments for fear of coming across as a braggart, Shine Theory is about leaning into the idea of mutual abundance and how someone else's success doesn't take away your own. In fact, you get a boost. (para. 14)

- *No one cares about your failures as much as you do.* This is called the spotlight effect. Everyone is too focused on themselves to focus on you.
- *Be mindful of burnout.* Set boundaries to make sure you properly recover and can start your efforts again. Remember, taxing projects are

both a marathon and a sprint. You can't sprint if you've just completed a marathon.

- *Believe in the possibility of future success.* This one really motivates me. Right now things aren't the best, but things have improved in the past. What stops them from improving now? I even like looking at job advertisements; the odds are low I will get the job, but the potential is there. The odds were low when I got all my other jobs too.

Why is it hard to have compassion for ourselves when we often have compassion for other people? Chris Germer contends that "self-compassion is our capacity to comfort and soothe ourselves, to motivate ourselves with encouragement, and to connect with innate compassion for others" (Mead, 2019, para. 15). Self-compassion helps us grow in the context of our relationships with others. You cannot have compassion for others without compassion for yourself, in my opinion. Less controversially, the more compassion you have for yourself, the more compassion you will have for others.

Clinical studies demonstrate that increased self-compassion is related to lower levels of anxiety and depression, decreased cortisol levels (cortisol contributes to stress), and higher optimism, curiosity, and self-initiative. Self-compassion is related to improved interpersonal relationships.

If you go through a failure, don't tell yourself it's your fault. Maybe it is, and maybe it isn't. Putting blame on yourself will not help you move forward from the failure. And that's what you have to do—whether you like it or not. If you find yourself spiraling from "failure," ask yourself the following:

- How would you treat a friend going through your situation?
- What do you want, and how does your "failure" relate to your desires?
- Turn yourself into a "criticizer," "criticized observer" and "compassionate observer," and describe your situation from each of these perspectives.

Birgit Ohlin (2016) writes:

If you were to go on a journey with someone for several decades, how important would the relationship between the two of you be?...Wouldn't you make an effort to ensure you got along well? Wouldn't you want to make sure the relationship between the two of you was positive and supportive?...The journey of life, the one we're all on right now, isn't so different from that hypo-thetical journey. Except rather than spending time with another person, our constant companion is the voice inside our heads. (para. 1-3)

I mentioned before that the way we perceive a situation is never truly objective. We all have our different inter-pretative styles of the truth. Accept that you are not perfect; there is potential for growth in every mistake. Ohlin (2016, para. 20) recalls the instructions when entering an airplane: "Put on your own oxygen mask first before helping anyone else."

Self-compassion means not only treating yourself like a friend but recognizing your own limitations. Try the following steps to foster your self-compassion:

- *Practice forgiveness.* Don't punish yourself for making mistakes because you would not punish your friends for the same. Forgiveness is not a one-time act but a life-long process. Remember, you do not need to be a certain way to be worthy of love.
- *Adopt a growth mindset.* I spoke about this in detail in Chapter 4. In summary, you should "embrace rather than avoid challenges" (Ohlin,

2016, para. 31). Find inspiration and strength among others, instead of feeling threatened.

- *Express gratitude.* Focusing on your blessings shows a gentler inner voice. It turns us away from our shortcomings and outward to the world. The world is beautiful enough for us to pay attention to it.

- *Find the right level of generosity.* All of us are givers, takers, or matchers. If you're a giver, know that the selfless approach may be unsuccessful in the long term. Be aware of your own needs before helping others. Being aware of yourself may let you have more fun in your generosity as well.

- *Be mindful.* Tend to the things that are happening in your life. In Heidegger's terms, turn your Care to your Lifeworld. For Heidegger (1962, p. 56), "having to do with something, producing something, attending to something and looking after it, making use of something, giving something up and letting it go, undertaking, accomplishing, evincing, interrogating, considering, discussing, determining" are all examples of Care (or things we can do to not cause anxiety).

I have failed in more ways than just with my money. Have you failed in relationships? I won't even get started on that one. But—you know—I would not be writing this book if I had not failed at something; I have something to show for my failure. Confucius states, "By three methods we may learn wisdom: First, by reflection, which is noblest; Second, by imitation, which is easiest; and third by experience, which is the bitterest" ("Confucius quotes," 2022). I am relating to you my wisdom by experience; yes, it is bitter, but it is a good lesson (for me and for you). You might not need to go through that, or maybe you already have.

I don't want people to fail like me. Not everyone needs to know the lessons I learned. If you can read this chapter and say, "I can move on from failure; I can keep an open mind to what 'success' means," then that's enough. Don't plunge yourself into the void to see what's in it (as Nietzsche warns: be careful what stares back at you in that void). It's hard enough to get through this forest, but we're almost out. Do you see the sun peeking through the trees? There! There's a clearing up ahead and the village we're going to. In this place, you can test out the new strategies you learned and see if your newfound self-confidence makes things significantly easier. I bet it will. If you still need a boost, read on in the next chapter.

9

QUICK TRICKS FOR AN INSTANT
SELF-CONFIDENCE BOOST

I think you're ready to bring it all together. Your mind has been "widening;" you learned new tips. New ideas. New *tricks*. You have a sense of how to be a more self-confident man, but you're still not sure. After all, I haven't even talked that much about masculinity, starting a family, or supporting someone. I vaguely talked about men's responsibility to ourselves and society. The fact is, women are different in some qualitative ways to men, though they're our equal. I'm partial to the works of the feminist writers Luce Irigaray and bell hooks, who emphasize the sexual difference between men and women; the latter of whom declares that you have to love men to her fellow feminists. I reject the notion that men and women are identical, but we complement each other in ways that are profound, if not divine. We also have similar motivations independent of our relationships to each other: love, success, and prestige (in one way or another). Many of the tips in this book for men are applicable to women. But what is a self-confident woman? A self-confident woman can be confident in a business career or as a homemaker. A self-confident man has expectations of himself from society; rarely is he confident at home (sometimes he is, if that partnership works for him). Often, a self-confident man is exploring what the world has to offer. He has to earn things; he has to take things for himself. He has to make a difference. Once in a while, he has to challenge authority.

The idea of what a man is changes with the times, and I don't want to dredge up the argument of whether this change is good now. But you are a man (most likely), reading this book, and you want to become more confident. Simple as that. The anthropology of masculinity is less interesting to you than gaining confidence (as it is to me). Women appreciate things in men that are timeless. In a word, these features of men are "perennial" (like flowers that come up every year). These features include strength, which is not only physical but spiritual (recall that Nietzsche, physically, was a weakling). They include honor, one aspect of which is keeping your word. They include social standing, which varies from professionals to artists; you can be attractive as a vagabond (with the right mindset). Since being a man is perennial, it is also ineffable. As much as I lay out these features that are common to men, you will find exceptions. Like Friedrich Nietzsche, Mahatma Gandhi was a small man, and he led his country to independence. Gandhi displayed strength in the face of adversity that I probably could not muster. The "essence" of what being a man is changes, but there *is* an essence. Tap into that essence if you want to gain the self-confidence befitting your sex.

Beyond that, though, there are some simple tips and tricks to round everything out. Some of these are extremely straightforward, and all of them are worth trying. I describe them in this chapter.

- *Sit up straight.* A Harvard study demonstrated that "people who were told to sit up straight were more likely to believe thoughts they wrote down in that posture" related to their qualifications for work. Meanwhile, those who were slumped over were less likely to believe in their own qualifications ("Body posture affects…," 2009, para. 1). It is not just what you say, but the way you say it that matters; moreover, our posture affects how we think about ourselves. Simply looking more confident will make you feel more confident.

An actress told me that men do push-ups before their scene to emphasize their pectorals. Do some push-ups.

- *Visualize yourself doing well.* Is there a link between mind and matter? Who knows; but what is known is that a positive attitude is correlated with more success, and one way to get your brain down that avenue is to picture it. As Jillian Kramer (2016, para. 2) states, "The mind takes cues from internal meditations." Something may be easier to achieve if you can see its mechanisms play out in your head.
- *Read positive notes about yourself.* Someone has written something nice about you. I know someone has written something nice about me, and I didn't always deserve it. I forget that I contributed to big projects with dollar signs attached, to scientific studies, and the like. I have publications, though they're marginal in my field. I was always impressed by how my supervisors characterized me; it was a positivity I didn't see in myself until I became a more self-confident man.
- *Smile.* "Smiling sends a straight-shot message to your brain to perk up," writes Kramer (2o16, para. 3) Moreover, "Smiling is contagious" (Kramer, 2016, para. 3). It might not only make

you feel better, but the people around you as well. That's enough to turn around a day.

- *Repeat a mantra.* A mantra is a catchphrase that is easy to say and remember, of which the repetition may ground us into what really matters. Science fiction nerds may recall Paul Atredies' mantra from *Dune* ("Quote from Frank…," 2022):

Fear is the mind-killer. Fear is the little-death that brings total obliteration. I will face my fear. I will permit it to pass over me and through me. And when it has gone past I will turn the inner eye to see its path. Where the fear has gone there will be nothing. Only I will remain.

This may be a mouthful, so try something like, "I've done this before, I can do it again" (or whatever it is that peps you up during a difficult moment).

- *Phone a friend.* Talking is therapeutic and—as I described in the last chapter—involved in emotional regulation. If you have someone you consider a confidant, don't let them stew away by themselves. Take the initiative and talk.
- *Act as if you are where you want to be.* This is complicated, and some of the following tips

become more complicated, but you basically want to "fake it until you make it" on a cosmic level. I don't know enough to preclude or include the idea that what you visualize comes true on Earth. What is absolutely true is most of our lives are intersubjective; therefore, projecting confidence (even if you don't have it) will make people more confident in you, thereby giving you more confidence.

- *Read your LinkedIn profile.* Related to my third point, go over your accomplishments, but from your own perspective. I have a three-page resume. That's as long as it should get before it turns into a CV. I'm surprised I was able to fill that much, and I like how I had to cut stuff out to make it three pages. Remember that you've done things no one else has. That's true by definition. Some people did similar things differently.

- *"Trick your mind" into thinking apprehension is excitement.* This tip is relatively complicated. Alison Brooks (2014, p. 1144) describes how "anxiety drains working memory capacity, decreases self-confidence, and harms performance." However, anxiety has what is called "arousal congruency" with excitement, which is related to similar performance issues but at a much lower scale. That is, you can perform a presentation well if you are excited; this is the same with anxiety—but you're more likely to perform it well if you're just excited. Brooks also points out that it is easier to go from arousal-congruent states than from states of high arousal to low arousal. That means that it is easier to go from anxious to excited than it is from anxious to calm. If you want to retain some of the benefits of excitement without the downsides of anxiety, just tell your brain you're not anxious, only excited.

- *Do yoga (or stretch).* I'm partial to yoga. I can't tell you why. Okay, maybe I can tell you why; I can't really meditate. Despite my exaltation of meditation in this book, I can't do it. I certainly know people it works for, and the literature describes its efficacy. What I can do is yoga, which puts you into a similar state as meditation (the two are related). Yoga lowers your heart rate and your breathing. After a session of yoga (trust me, just get started, it's easy once you're five minutes in), you'll feel like you've successfully meditated. I'm not misleading you; I meditate with my body first until my mind catches up with it.

- *Play empowering music.* I described how I like Wagner. Perhaps you like Grandmaster Flash and the Furious Five's 1982 hit song "The Message." Maybe you like Lou Reed's album *Street Hassle.* These examples of music are all empowering in their own ways. Music is really personal, so I won't make any more recommendations. Music takes you away from suffering because it mimics the Will that motivates all of life, per Schopenhauer.

- *Dress for success.* As a man, this could not be a more important point to building self-confidence. How to dress well for a man requires its own book, and plenty of resources exist already. I will only add my two cents, which are that it is always better to be dressed up than dressed down. You should invest in at least one suit (I recommend blue). A man requires one accessory: a wristwatch. Everything else is optional. You should work out because you will always look better, no matter your body type.

- *Celebrate your accomplishments!* I already mentioned this as a tip in previous chapters, but you have to train your mind (through neuroplasticity) to focus on the positive, so I think it bears repeating (did someone say something about *bears*? I think we're almost out of the forest!). Even if it feels hokey, invite your friends along for your celebrations. A friendship between men should be fostered, and more feelings should be expressed than is currently commonly accepted.

- *Read books (including this one).* I included this point because I didn't want to end on 13 points. That being said, what does reading books have to do with self-confidence? I described earlier that women look for perennial traits in men. One of these traits, broadly speaking, is competence. Books teach you things; they take you away to faraway worlds or teach you to fix motorcycles. Reading trains your brain, even if the book tells you nothing. In a world that is becoming increasingly uninterested in reading (as our attention span shrinks to the length of a Tik-Tok video), it may become a masculine feature to own a dog-eared copy of G.W.F. Hegel's *Phenomenology of Spirit.* Maybe not, but one can dream.

I think you're well on your way to getting out of this forest. Can you believe it? You took the path least traveled, and you met *me*; I guess in a way I should apologize for that. At the same time, some people pay good money to be in my company, so I hope escorting you through the forest is not for naught (sorry for the double negative).

There's the village down below! It has everything you're looking for: an inn, a tavern (save that activity for the evening), a general store, a blacksmith, and a pharmacy (where they sell the health potions). Everyone you want to talk to is here; maybe even a lass you can introduce yourself to. The only thing they don't have is a place to charge your phone. Are you okay unplugging for a while?

CONCLUSION

What is a self-confident man? A self-confident man is, first and foremost, a man. A man has a responsibility to other people, namely his family, friends, colleagues, and associates, probably in that order. A man also has a responsibility for the suffering he sees among strangers; a man will come to your aid if you need it. Often the assailant is another man, but you get the idea.

A self-confident man is a man who lives life for its intrinsic value. What this means is that you value the process more than the outcome; you know that you matter whether or not you succeed. A self-confident man does not rely on external validation. Isaac Newton and Gottfried Liebnitz developed calculus simultaneously, and they bickered only about the correct notation to use; they did not cry over the muddled reception of their theories. Both men were perfectly confident in their discovery.

A self-confident man goes about his life whether he is Newton or a store clerk, like I was. Ben was a barman; now, he sells buildings that house the bars he used to work at. What does he attribute to his success? Projecting confidence until he got more and more small wins. Before you know it, your wins get bigger.

Am I a self-confident man? I would think so. Confidence comes in many forms—it is not *arrogance*—but one thing all confidence displays is an ability to take up space that you deserve to be in. I deserve to be here, I believe. I deserve that you read my words, even if you don't know me. I'm confident enough to say that it does not bother me if you don't believe what I say because I strongly believe that you *should* believe what I say. I know, in fact, that you should believe it, but everyone interprets truth differently. That's the beauty of life. Not everyone takes the road less traveled by, but you did. Are you going to take these lessons down a new road, or are you going to take the same exit out to the McDonalds? The choice is yours, my friend; I wish you the best of luck in materializing the man that you deserve to be.

REFERENCES

10 tips to overcome self-doubt (2020). Eugene Therapy. eugenetherapy.-com/article/overcome-self-doubt

Ambrisino, B. (2014). *Hell is other people ... misquoting philosophers.* Vox. vox.com/2014/11/17/7229547/philosophy-quotes-misunderstood-wittgenstein-sartre-descartes.

Aurelius, M. (2012). *Meditations.* Oxford University Press.

Bliss, J. (2014). *The importance of male self-love.* Good Men Project. goodmenproject.com/featured-content/j1b-ballers-of-the-heart-the-importance-of-male-self-love

Body posture affects confidence in your own thoughts, study finds (2009). ScienceDaily. sciencedaily.com/releases/2009/10/091005111627.htm.

Britton, J. (2019). *5 steps to communicate your needs to your friends (without feeling needy).* Yellow Co. archive.yellowco.co/blog/2019/03/18/5-steps-communicate-needs-friends-without-feeling-needy

Brooks, A. (2014). Get excited: Reappraising pre-performance anxiety as excitement. *Journal of Experimental Psychology* 143(3), 1144-1158.

Brooten-Brooks, M. (2022). *What is boundary setting?* VeryWell Health. verywellhealth.com/setting-boundaries-5208802

Carson, T. (2010). Kant and the absolute prohibition against lying. *Lying and deception: Theory and practice.* Oxford University Press.

Cherry, K. (2021a, September 3). *How to stop being a people-pleaser.* Very Well Mind. verywellmind.com/how-to-stop-being-a-people-pleaser-5184412

Cherry, K. (2021b, April 19). *What is mindset and why it matters.* Very-Well Mind. verywellmind.com/what-is-a-mindset-2795025

Cherry, K. (2022, February 14). *What is self-concept?* VeryWell Mind. verywellmind.com/what-is-self-concept-2795865

Chesak, J. (2018). *The no BS guide to protecting your email space.* Health-Line. healthline.com/health/mental-health/set-boundaries

Cicero, M. (1923). *De senectute de amicitia de divinatione*. Harvard University Press.

Clarke, J. (2021). *Healthy ways to celebrate success*. VeryWell Mind. verywellmind.com/healthy-ways-to-celebrate-success-4163887

Confucius quotes (2022). BrainyQuote. brainyquote.com/quotes/confucius_131984

Coval, K. (2012). *Slingshots: A hip-hop poetica*. EM Press.

Cutruzzula, K. (2020). *How to move on after failure—and rebuild your confidence*. TED Conferences, LLC., ideas.ted.com/how-to-move-on-after-failure-and-rebuild-confidence-erika-hamden

De Waal, C. (2005). *On pragmatism*. Wadsworth.

Eatough, E. (2022). *How to say no to others (and why you shouldn't feel guilty)*. BetterUp. betterup.com/blog/how-to-say-no

Edberg, H. (2020). *How to overcome failure: 9 powerful habits*. The Positivity Blog. positivityblog.com/how-to-overcome-failure

Eddins, R. (2020). *A man's guide to practicing self-love*. Eddins Counseling Group. eddinscounseling.com/mans-guide-to-self-love

English standard Bible (2001). Crossway Bibles. esv.literalword.com

Ferebee, A. (2022). *The ultimate guide to practicing self-love for men*. Knowledge for Men. knowledgeformen.com/self-love-for-men

Frost, R. (2022). *The road not taken*. Poetry Foundation. poetryfoundation.org/poems/44272/the-road-not-taken

Gajanan, M. (2016). *A brief history of Mother Teresa's complicated faith*. Time. time.com/4476076/mother-teresas-faith-history

Gammill, T. et al. (1994). The raincoats. *Seinfeld*. NBC.

Georgiou, S. (1970). Hard-headed woman. *Tea for the tillerman*. Universal UMC.

Gray, J. (2002). *Straw dogs: Thoughts on humans and other animals*. Granta.

Gray, J. (2016). *How to fiercely protect your time*. Jordan Gray Consulting. jordangrayconsulting.com/how-to-fiercely-protect-your-time

Guttman, J. (2019). *The relationship with yourself*. Psychology Today. psychologytoday.com/us/blog/sustainable-life-satisfaction/201906/the-relationship-yourself

Harris, N. (2022). *Confidence vs. self-efficacy*. LaTrobe University. latrobe.edu.au/nest/confidence-versus-self-efficacy

Heidegger, M. (1962). *Being and time*. Blackwell.

Hendricksen, E. (2017). *Nine ways to fight imposter syndrome*. Psychology Today. psychologytoday.com/us/blog/how-be-your-self/201708/nine-ways-fight-impostor-syndrome

Henry Ford quotes (2022). GoodReads. goodreads.com/quotes/978-whether-you-think-you-can-or-you-think-you-can-t--you-re

Holland, K. (2020). *Positive self-talk: How talking to yourself is a good thing*. HealthLine. healthline.com/health/positive-self-talk

hooks, b. (1996). *Reel to real*. Routledge.

How to protect your energy (2022). Achieve Medical Center. achievemedicalcenter.com/blog-post/how-to-protect-your-energy

Howard, L. (2017). *How to feel comfortable asking for what you need in a relationship*. Bustle. bustle.com/p/how-to-feel-more-comfortable-asking-for-what-you-need-in-a-relationship-59044

Imposter syndrome (2022). Psychology Today. psychologytoday.com/us/basics/imposter-syndrome

Imposter syndrome: What it is and how to overcome it (2022). The Cleveland Clinic. health.clevelandclinic.org/a-psychologist-explains-how-to-deal-with-imposter-syndrome

Jagger, M. & Richards, K. (1969). You can't always get what you want. *Let it bleed*. ABKCO Music & Records.

Kelly, Y. et al. (2018). Social media use and adolescent mental health: Findings from the UK millennium cohort study. *Lancet 6*.

Kristenson, S. (2022). *8 SMART goals examples for building more confidence*. Develop Good Habits. developgoodhabits.com/smart-goals-confidence

Kurasawa, A. (1950). *Rashomon*. Daiei Films.

Lachmann, S. (2013). *10 sources of low self esteem*. Psychology Today. psychologytoday.com/us/blog/me-we/201312/10-sources-low-self-esteem

Lotz, C. (2022). *Being - being and beings*. Sacramentum Mundi Online. referenceworks.brillonline.com/entries/sacramentum-mundi/being-being-and-beings-COM_000441

Lucas, G. (1977). *Star Wars*. Lucasfilms.

MacKaye, I. (1989). Waiting room. *Thirteen songs*. Dischord Records.

Mandel, M. (2022). *How to grow from mistakes and stop beating yourself up.* TinyBuddha. tinybuddha.com/blog/how-to-grow-from-mistakes-and-stop-beating-yourself-up/

Marcus Aurelius quotes (2022). GoodReads. goodreads.com/author/quotes/17212.Marcus_Aurelius

Markway, B. (2018). *Why self-confidence is more important than you think.* Psychology Today. psychologytoday.com/us/blog/shyness-is-nice/201809/why-self-confidence-is-more-important-you-think

Marshall, C. (2017). *Try again. Fail again. Fail Better.* Goethe Institute. goethe.de/ins/us/en/sta/los/bib/feh/21891928.html

Mead, E. (2019). *What is mindful self-compassion?* Positive Psychology. positivepsychology.com/mindful-self-compassion

Meline, J. (2002). Delorean. *Fantastic damage.* Def Jux.

Merriam-Webster. (n.d.). Self love. In *Merriam-Webster.com dictionary.* Retrieved August 31, 2022, from merriam-webster.com/dictionary/self-love

Milius, J. (1982). *Conan the Barbarian.* Universal Pictures.

Morin, A. (2021). *Healthy coping skills for uncomfortable emotions.* Very-Well Mind. verywellmind.com/forty-healthy-coping-skills-4586742

Morrissey, S. & Marr, J. (1986). Ask. *Ask.* Rough Trade Records.

Nietzsche, F. (1974) *The gay science.* Vintage.

Peirce, C. (1955). *Philosophical writings of Peirce.* Dover.

Pillay, H. (2014). *Why it's important to know your strengths and weaknesses.* Leaderonmics. leaderonomics.com/articles/personal/why-its-important-to-know-your-strengths-and-weaknesses

Plato. (1968). *The Republic.* Basic Books.

Plato. (2001). *Symposium.* University of Chicago Press.

Quote by Frank Herbet (2022). GoodReads. goodreads.com/quotes/2-i-must-not-fear-fear-is-the-mind-killer-fear-is

Ralph Waldo Emerson quotes about confidence (2022). AZQuotes. azquotes.com/author/4490-Ralph_Waldo_Emerson/tag/confidence

Ravenscraft, E. (2019). *Practical ways to improve your self-confidence (and why you should).* The New York Times. nytimes.-

com/2019/06/03/smarter-living/how-to-improve-self-confi-dence.html

Reed, L. (1970). Head held high. *Loaded*. Cottitlon Records.

Robertson, W. (2003). 'Oh, what a tangled web we weave, when first we practice to deceive!' (Sir Walter Scott, 1808). *Journal of veterinary and human toxicology* 45(2), 112-113.

Robbins, T. (2022). *The ultimate guide to limiting beliefs*. Robbins Research International, Inc. tonyrobbins.com/limiting-beliefs-guide

Russell, B. (1967). *The history of western philosophy*. Simon & Schuster.

Ohlin, B. (2016). *5 steps to develop self-compassion & overcome your inner critic*. Positive Psychology. positivepsychology.com/self-compassion-5-steps

Olsen, A. (2016). Intern. *My Woman*. Blooming Jazz Records.

Sartre, J. (1943). *Being and nothingness*. Éditions Gallimard, Philosophical Library.

Schopenhauer, A. (1969). *The world as will and representation*. Dover.

Scott, E. (2021). *Avoidance coping and why it creates additional stress*. Very-Well Mind. verywellmind.com/avoidance-coping-and-stress-4137836

Scott, E. (2022). *The toxic effects of negative self-talk*. VeryWell Mind. verywellmind.com/negative-self-talk-and-how-it-affects-us-4161304

Self-love for men (2020). Medium. selffirst.medium.com/self-love-for-men-d58d7dac9cac

Self-love index (2022). The Body Shop International Limited. thebodyshop.com/en-gb/about-us/activism/self-love/self-love index/a/a00043

Seneca the Younger quote (2022). LibQuotes. libquotes.com/seneca/quote/lbr2w0c

Sloane, P. (2022). *Welcome failure*. Lifehack. lifehack.org/articles/work/welcome-failure.html

Smith, R. & Harte, V. (2021). *10 famous people who raised their self-esteem*. Dummies. dummies.com/article/body-mind-spirit/emotional-health-psychology/emotional-health/general-emotional-health/10-famous-people-who-raised-their-self-esteem-145436

Sowell, T. (1998). *Late-talking children*. Basic books.

Stone, K. (2019). *Communicating your needs isn't selfish, it's selfless*. Rewire. rewire.org/communicating-needs-selfless

Sutton, J. (2021). *18 best growth mindset activities, worksheets, and questions*. Positive Psychology. positivepsychology.com/growth-mindset.

Taleb, N. (2012). *Antifragile: Things that gain from disorder*. Random House.

Tardanico, S. (2012). *Five ways to make peace with failure*. Forbes. forbes.com/sites/susantardanico/2012/09/27/five-ways-to-make-peace-with-failure/?sh=367b69703640.

Van Dyke, K. (2021). *Feeling stuck? How to express your feelings*. Psych-Central. psychcentral.com/lib/feeling-stuck-how-to-express-your-feelings#sharing-your-feelings

Veale, J. (1974). The beginning of wisdom is the ability to call things by their right names. Confucius. *The Journal of the American Academy of Gold Foil Operators* 17(2).

Warhol, A. (1977). *The philosophy of Andy Warhol: from A to B and back again*. Harcourt Brace Jovanovich.

Waters, S. (2022). *Perfectionism isn't a virtue (and doesn't help with well-being, either)*. BetterUp. betterup.com/blog/perfectionism?hsLang=en.

Wignall, N. (2019). *Growth mindset: The surprising psychology of self-belief*. Nuthymia, LLC. nickwignall.com/growth-mindset

Wooll, M. (2022). *Wondering what you're good at? Here are 10 ways to find out*. BetterUp. betterup.com/blog/how-to-find-what-you-are-good-at.

Printed in Great Britain
by Amazon